Quotes on p. 5 are reproduced from Collins 2004
with kind permission from Tessler Agency.

First published in 2016
by Jessica Kingsley Publishers
73 Collier Street
London N1 9BE, UK
and
400 Market Street, Suite 400
Philadelphia, PA 19106, USA

www.jkp.com

Library of Congress Cataloging in Publication Data
McKibbin, Karen.
Life on the autism spectrum : a guide for girls and women
/ Karen McKibbin ; foreword by Tony Attwood.
pages cm
Includes index.
ISBN 978-1-84905-747-9 (alk. paper)
1. Autistic people--Life skills guides. 2. Girls--Life skills guides. 3.
Young women with disabilities--Life skills guides. I. Title.
RC553.A88M392 2016
616.85'882--dc23
2015016763

British Library Cataloguing in Publication Data
A CIP catalogue record for this book is available from the British Library

ISBN 978 1 84905 747 9
eISBN 978 1 78450 193 8

Printed and bound in the United States

"McKibbin's solid research and clinical experiences work together in this book to give voice and support to countless autistic and Aspie females who have been misdiagnosed, misunderstood, or simply missed altogether. Thank you, Dr. McKibbin!"

—*Liane Holliday Willey, EdD, author of* Pretending to be Normal *and* Safety Skills for Asperger Women

"*Life on the Autism Spectrum: A Guide for Girls and Women* is a natural and welcome progression in the growing catalog of literature aimed at understanding the complexities of females with Asperger's."

—*Rudy Simone, author of* Aspergirls *and* Aunt Aspie's Weapon of Mass Instruction

"Karen has contributed a valuable addition to the growing wealth of knowledge about the female autistic profile. With real-life examples and tips for living well, this book will support autistic women to gain the real sense of our own identity that we all need."

—*Sarah Hendrickx, Autistic Adult and Autism Specialist, author of* Women and Girls with ASD: Understanding Life Experiences from Early Childhood to Old Age

"This book provides a refreshing and empowering look at the female experience of autism spectrum disorders throughout the life span. Dr. McKibbin's compassionate insights on the challenges and gifts unique to girls and women on the spectrum will leave readers inspired. This is a refreshing opportunity for readers to shift their focus from how autism sets individuals apart to truly appreciating the common threads that bind us together. Truly, a must read."

—*Erin Moran, Psy.D., Clinical Psychologist*

LIFE ON THE
AUTISM
SPECTRUM

A Guide for Girls and Women

Karen McKibbin   Foreword by Tony Attwood

Jessica Kingsley *Publishers*
London and Philadelphia

This book is dedicated to all the incredible women who contributed to it. It would not have been possible without you.

Thank you to all my friends and family who supported me in making this book possible.

Think of it: a disability is usually defined in terms of what is missing… But Autism…is as much about what is abundant as what is missing, an over-expression of the very traits that make our species unique.

Autists are the ultimate square pegs, and the problem with pounding a square peg into a round hole is not that the hammering is hard work. It's that you're destroying the peg.

Paul Collins

CONTENTS

FOREWORD

Dr. Tony Attwood

Life on the autism spectrum is not easy for girls and women. Although they may have the same profile of characteristics as males, they often adjust to that profile in a different way, and also have different social and society expectations. Thus, girls and women need their own guide, and Karen's book is the authoritative guide.

In comparison to boys, girls and women who have an ASD use more constructive coping and adjustment strategies to effectively camouflage their confusion in social situations. They may achieve superficial social success by imitation, or by avoiding engagement in interpersonal situations by escaping into an alternative world of fantasy or nature.

The young girl with ASD can become an avid observer of other children and intellectually analyse and determine what to do in social situations: learning to copy or imitate other girls, or adopting an alternative persona and "acting" someone who can succeed in social situations. She becomes a social "chameleon." Alternatively, some girls escape into imagination and create an alternative world. They constructively avoid social interactions and play with other children, choosing instead to engage in solitary play, developing artistic and musical abilities, avidly reading fiction or spending time enjoying being with pets and animals.

One of the first signs of ASD in girls can be extremely intense emotions, especially distress, and an inability to be comforted by affection, or calmed by reasoning or distraction. Additional aspects can be sensory sensitivity, especially tactile and auditory sensitivity, resistance to change, and the development of routines and rituals. Language abilities can include problems with the "art of conversation" and a tendency to be pedantic or mute in social situations. Parents notice that their daughter may not identify with or want to play cooperatively with her female peers. She may consider that the play of other girls is stupid, boring and inexplicable, and prefer to play alone so that she can do things her own way. When she does play with her peers, she may be domineering and authoritarian. Her play interests can also be different to other girls her age. She may prefer non-gender specific toys such as Lego®, or playing with toys more often associated with boys, such as construction sets and vehicles.

Some girls who have an ASD seem uninterested in or oblivious of the latest craze for girls of their age, and pursue their own idiosyncratic interest. When they do have gender associated interests, such as a passion for horses, it is to an intensity and degree that is unusual. They may be averse to the concept of femininity, choosing not to wear the latest fashions or collect the popular toys to be "cool." They may well prefer to be with and play with boys, whose play is more constructive and adventurous, rather than emotional and conversational. They may enjoy being perceived as "tomboys." In contrast, an alternative characteristic is to avidly observe and analyse the play of other girls, perhaps identifying someone who is socially successful and popular, and adopting that person's persona by mimicking speech patterns, phrases, body language and even clothing and interests. The girl becomes someone else, someone who would be accepted and not recognized as different. She then learns how to act in social situations, a strategy so successful that people may not be aware that the social abilities were a performance, achieved by intellect and imitation rather than intuition and inspiration.

If she does have friendships, they are likely to be quite intense and exclusively focused on one other girl, who may provide guidance for her in social situations at school, and who has tolerance and compassion for her eccentric characteristics. In return, the girl with ASD is a loyal and helpful friend, rarely interested in the "backbiting," competitive behaviour of her gender peers.

During childhood and adolescence, some girls with ASD are renowned for being extremely well behaved and compliant in class so as not to be noticed or recognized as different by the teacher or other children. They may then supress their social confusion in silence and isolation, yet be a very different character at home. The "mask" is removed, and the girl may use passive-aggressive behaviour such as tantrums, threats and non-compliance to control her social experiences with her family. She has two characters, the meek, compliant schoolgirl, and the defiant, argumentative and emotionally volatile daughter.

While some adolescent girls with ASD can observe, analyse and imitate the social abilities of peers as a way of achieving friendships and inclusion, in the later teenage years, if this strategy is not leading to social inclusion and success, there can be a complete reversal of the role of "goody two shoes."

The girl may make a conscious decision to deliberately break the social conventions and engage in risky and provocative behaviour, such as promiscuity and drug taking, to the great distress of her parents and teachers.

Thus, we need to identify as early as possible girls who have an ASD level 1 (Asperger's syndrome) and to develop and design strategies to help them acquire social knowledge, acceptance and inclusion. Karen has used her extensive clinical experience and insight, as well as compassion, to write the definitive guide to the key characteristics, adjustments and behaviours associated with the female expression of ASD. This is the primary source for guidance for parents and professionals, and also for girls and women who have Asperger's syndrome.

Dr. Tony Attwood
Minds and Hearts Clinic
Brisbane

INTRODUCTION

Alison is an eight-year-old girl. She's standing alone at recess watching everyone else in her class play together and have fun. For them, it's fun to be social. It is energizing, relaxing, motivating. It helps them get through the rest of the day. But not for Alison. For her, recess is confusing, overwhelming, and she's just not sure how to fit in. She watches the other girls from her class and what they do. She goes home and practices "acting" this way with others so she can maybe make a friend tomorrow by doing what they all do. But it never quite works. The other girls get frustrated with her, avoid her, and when they get fed up, they call her names and play jokes on her. All she wants is to feel like she belongs, but nothing she ever does seems to make it easier. Each day she hopes that she's able to find that "secret ingredient" that will earn her a friend. But every day is met with another frustration and another failure. So she withdraws from others. The teachers don't notice, they see her as "quirky" and "shy." They don't see her as a behavior problem because she isn't one. So she's left alone, isolated, and misunderstood.

At home, while she feels like this is her safe haven, the expectations of her are still overwhelming. Why does she have to eat only one brand of chicken nuggets? Why won't she eat the same foods as everyone else? So many foods seem overwhelming to her, so many sounds and textures make her skin and ears feel like they are going into overdrive, like she wants to crawl out of her own skin to get away from it all. And her family also doesn't understand why doing things at the last minute is so hard for her. For them, going out to eat dinner at a new restaurant is a "treat," but for her it's a nightmare. Not only is it a change to her daily routine, but there's no warning, and then she has to navigate how to survive the smells, the choices, the foods, and the people there. By the time she gets home, she's so exhausted and overwhelmed that she often starts to scream and cry, throwing herself to the ground. She can't hear what people are saying to her when she feels like this and nothing feels like it's going to calm her down. Her body and mind are so overloaded that she just has to lose control in order to reset herself in some way.

Homework feels like such a challenge too. Not because she doesn't understand it and not because she doesn't find it easy. But at the end of the school day, after trying to navigate all the other kids, trying to figure out why she doesn't seem to fit in, and working through the verbal overload of new information and trying to learn it all, she is just exhausted. The last thing she wants to do is sit down and do her homework. It's all work that she's already done in school, so why does she have to do it again when she knows it, and her teacher knows that she knows it too? It seems like such a pointless exercise. Refusing to do it always ends up in an argument with her mom too. Why can't anyone understand that all she wants is some time to decompress and relax, to recover from her day and from all the social expectations she's had to go through? Why are her parents so insistent that schoolwork must be finished before she can play? Her brother doesn't seem to have a problem with doing this, and this is brought to her attention almost every day. Why can't you just be more like your brother?

The one thing that gives Alison true joy and peace is being able to do what she truly loves. Being able to make up stories and tell them to her parents, or anyone who might listen (usually adults) helps her feel good about herself, as though she has a true gift that she can share with others and that will be appreciated. She also loves to draw out her characters so she can feel as though they are coming to life for her. This is where her passion, her true happiness and her confidence lie. Where she feels the best about herself. If only the rest of her day could feel as good for her as the time she is able to spend doing what she loves the most.

Alison walks into a psychologist's office. She is now 38 years old and has set up an appointment with a psychologist who says she specializes in working with individuals on the autism spectrum. She has recently been told that her niece, who is nine years old, has Asperger's and she wants to understand why. Of all the relationships that Alison has had in her life, her niece is the only person that she understands—and who seems to understand her. How could she have a "disorder?"

Alison has learned throughout her life to be very untrusting of doctors, psychologists, and psychiatrists. She has seen many "professionals" throughout her life, none of whom have understood her or provided her with any support. They have given her plenty of labels—depressed, anxious, suicidal, bipolar, borderline personality disorder... The list goes on. And for each of those labels she's been given, a cocktail of medications has been provided with them. Medications are supposed to "help her feel better" and "help her learn to cope better with her difficulties and problems." But all of these medications have given her a myriad of problems— sleep problems, explosions in her behaviors, feeling like she's trudging through a fog, feeling numbed, miserable, hopeless...alone.

Throughout her life, Alison has struggled in so many areas. She left school without good grades, not because she isn't smart, but because the subjects never motivated her. She has always had a love and a passion for animals—for caring for them, helping them and understanding them in a way that no one else seems to be able to. Alison has also struggled with keeping a job. Without the grades to get into a good training program to work with animals, she has had a number of jobs that haven't been successful—working as a waitress, a bar tender, a front desk person in hotels. All of these jobs have ended in frustration from her co-workers and inevitably some kind of emotional explosion from Alison, leaving her fired and without a good reason why (in her mind). There was one job she had a few years ago, which she loved, training guide dogs for children and adults. But this job was short-lived after she was propositioned by a co-worker who just wouldn't take "no" for an answer. Feeling terrified and unsafe, Alison never returned to her job and has been afraid to get another one ever since. She feels so isolated within her community. While she has a beautiful and wonderful niece with whom she has a very special and unique bond, she has not been able to have any other successful or long-standing relationship in her life. So, why all of a sudden, has someone decided that the one person in the world that she can relate to and can understand her has a "disorder?"

After leaving the psychologist's office she finally begins to understand why. After all this time of being so misunderstood and so alone in the world, Alison now knows why—she finally has an answer. Just like her niece, she too has Asperger's syndrome. As overwhelming and shocked as she feels with this news, she also knows that this has opened up doors for her that she never would have imagined. For the first time in as long as she can remember, she feels relief and feels as if there may finally be light at the end of her very dark tunnel.

Asperger's syndrome (AS) is thought of in many different ways. It is referred to as many things including "the invisible end of the spectrum" and "mild autism," although if you ask any person with Asperger's, they will rarely agree that their challenges are "mild." When you ask someone what they think of when you say the word "Asperger's" to them, they might say they think of *Rain Man*, or they might think of Sheldon Cooper (a character in the sitcom *The Big Bang Theory*), Einstein, or the actor Dan Aykroyd. But before we ask ourselves how accurate (or fair) those images and statements are, ask yourself another question – what do people think about when you say that a woman (or a girl) has Asperger's (AS)? Of course we have some incredible women with AS and high functioning autism (HFA) who have done truly amazing things in teaching us about what it's like to live with AS (Temple Grandin, Liane Holliday Willey, Rudy Simone to name a few). But outside the Asperger's community, how many people recognize these names, or are aware of the knowledge and unique experiences and insights that these women have to share?

The challenge is that, since autism was originally identified in the late 1940s, the history of autism and Asperger's has always been dominated by males. The criteria that we use today to diagnose autism spectrum disorders (ASDs) are based exclusively on boys. Rates of Asperger's at the time of writing are estimated to be between eight to ten males for every one female. This is being contested by many well-known professionals in the field, such as Dr. Tony Attwood who believes that the rate of Asperger's is significantly higher in females (about two males to each female)—women can just hide it better!

Understanding how Asperger's looks different in females can be difficult to explain. The core traits and characteristics of Asperger's are very similar in men and women, but it is the expression of these characteristics and how they are experienced that makes being a female with Asperger's unique. There are numerous theories on what causes these differences, from evolutionary to socially determined ones (although that's a subject for another book entirely!). It can be agreed, however, that regardless of the origins of these differences, they do exist in our world today and are a huge part of how we see, understand, interpret, and respond to the behaviors we see in others.

Whether we are looking at individuals with a diagnosis on the autism spectrum or neurotypicals (NTs) we can see there are an infinite number of differences between males and females that are expressed in many different ways. As a generalization across most cultures, boys will innately be more inclined to externalize difficult emotions. So when boys (or males) are angry, frustrated, feeling alienated, or confused, they will tend to act out in ways that will get them more immediate attention. The easiest way to get this attention is by engaging in behaviors like yelling, shouting, cursing, hitting, kicking, and throwing things. (When a book hits you on the head, it's hard not to notice and respond to that!) Girls, on the other hand, tend to retreat into themselves when these emotions become overwhelming to them. They internalize them and withdraw into themselves. People around them see them as cute and shy, certainly not a behavior problem or someone to be worried about.

There are many other behavioral differences between genders across our societies. For example, NT females tend to smile more often than men, which can make girls appear more appealing and attractive, friendlier, and more aware of social nuances and relationships. NT males will tend to interrupt others more often than women, and they can also appear more oblivious to the social cues given by others, which are provided to try and indicate that being interrupted is not always appreciated by others. When you combine these behaviors with the social–communication difficulties that exist within AS, you can begin to see how the expression of Asperger's can be so different between males and females, especially when so many differences between genders also exist within the NT population.

So the goal in writing this book is to help show that women with Asperger's are unique; while they can share many of the characteristics of their male counterparts, there are many differences that exist between them that are currently being overlooked and ignored. My hope is that this book will help to make the characteristics that are unique to women with Asperger's better understood by the families of girls and women on the autism spectrum and the professionals who work with them. I also hope that this book will serve to help girls and women with Asperger's to feel that they can better understand themselves and to see that there are many other women out in the world who are just like them.

Recently there has been a change in the way in which autism and Asperger's are diagnosed. Professionals can no longer provide a diagnosis of Asperger's disorder or Asperger's syndrome as they are now considered all to be part of the same spectrum. Instead, the label is "autism spectrum disorder," accompanied by a "severity level" which indicates how severe current symptoms are in terms of their impact on daily functioning. This specifier is designed to be changeable over time, as symptoms and severity can fluctuate. However, many individuals, both male and female, who have a previous diagnosis of Asperger's feel very strongly connected to this term and see it as an integral part of their identity.

For the purpose of this book, the term "Asperger's" will be used to refer to all individuals with Asperger's disorder and high functioning autism. Many individuals with these diagnoses currently accept and embrace the term "Asperger's" or "Aspie," which was coined by Dr. Tony Attwood in his book *Asperger's Syndrome: A Guide for Parents and Professionals*, published in 1998. Neither of these terms used in this book are meant to be derogatory, but are used in the same way as they are within the Asperger's community—as a way to identify themselves and embrace their unique individuality.

Just because you have a diagnosis does
not mean you have a disability.

1

THE SOCIAL WORLD AND COMMUNICATION

Each day Alison goes to school, she longs to find a friend. She doesn't need to feel like she's the most popular kid in school, but just to have one friend would be really nice. So, each day at recess, she watches her peers on the playground—how they play, how they interact with each other. At the end of the day, she goes home and replays these scenarios with her dolls in her room so that she can try to understand how to join in. Acceptance and pleasing others is so important to her. Even though she's shy and is learning that being by herself is often "safer" than to risk being bullied, frustrated, or outright rejected by her peers, Alison longs to make a friend and have someone to share her interests with. Her peers at school won't listen to her talk endlessly about animals and pets, which is mystifying to Alison because she knows so many fascinating facts about all kinds of animals. Why wouldn't other people want to know them too? Maybe if they just listened long enough, they would be amazed by the facts Alison knows and that would be the key to a lasting friendship.

One day, she decides she's going to try and join in and play with her peers at recess. Adults keep telling her that she should ask if she can play too, so she decides to try it.

And it works—they let her play! But they're running and shouting, and changing the rules and it's so loud and confusing that Alison just wants to scream! Why can't they just slow down? Why do they need to keep changing the rules? It's so overwhelming but she knows she can't freak out about it in front of everyone—then no one will ever talk to her again. So she quietly retreats and spends the rest of her day trying to recover—to figure it all out—to try and slow it down so it makes sense. The adults who see her just think that she's shy, which is good for Alison, because it allows her to be left alone.

Trying to decompress and understand the events at recess, coupled with trying to learn what is being taught in class is exhausting. Teachers keep thinking that she's not paying attention, or she's not doing things right, but they're not explaining all the work in a way that Alison can understand. The noise of recess is still ringing so loudly in her ears. By the time she gets home at the end of the day she just falls apart—she has no more energy for anything. Once she gets home, it can all come out—home is her haven, her safe place—and once it is all out of her system, she can continue with the rest of her evening. Even though she's calmed down, it still doesn't take much to upset her. Her energy and tolerance for anything are gone, and it won't be until the next day that she'll feel like her energy and tolerance are recharged so she can try again.

Alison also finds these challenges are the same when she has to go to annual family functions. Christmas is always the big one she can count on. Everyone is talking about a hundred different things all at once. It's so hard to follow even one conversation, let alone all of them at the same time. And the hardest part is that she has to "pretend" to be interested in them, even though no one seems to care about what she wants to say. Why is it okay for other people to interrupt her and then walk away when she's talking, but she's not allowed to do it when she is bored by other people? She gets so frustrated and eventually gets so overwhelmed that she screams as loud and hard as she can—that makes everyone go quiet! But then the consequences of this leave her feeling even more alone and misunderstood.

Since leaving school, Alison has tried to make connections and relationships with others in a variety of different settings. And while she hasn't had to endure the torment that she did in school, she has still found herself being taken advantage of by others. Having to do all the nasty jobs that others didn't want to do, being blamed for things that she didn't do. And even when she has been invited out on social occasions, everyone else seems to find enjoyment in such different ways to her—their interests, where they want to go, how they interact—they all just seem so different to what she wants to do. Her colleagues would want to go out and drink, dance, and make fools of themselves, while Alison wanted to find somewhere quiet so that she could spend time with someone whom she could share an intelligent conversation with. Nothing ever seemed to match up for her with the rest of the world.

Throughout her life, Alison has always struggled to engage successfully in conversations with others. Throughout her numerous jobs and attempts to join in with others in a social way, she has been continually frustrated by the seemingly pointless things that others around her insist on discussing—the weather, the weekend, vacation plans, gossip about celebrities that they've never met. The frustration of these seemingly pointless conversations causes Alison to prefer to be alone and avoid co-workers when she can. But she has found that most jobs require some form of communication. One thing that she has noticed irritates her co-workers more than her preference for talking about animals is when she tries to help them by correcting their mistakes and errors and pointing out when they're breaking the rules. It's difficult to understand why they get so irritated by this—after all, she's only trying to help. But inevitably it ends up with her being brought into her boss's office where she gets reprimanded and eventually told that the job "just isn't going to work out." She's learned over the years that walking away is always a better option than launching into an argument where she always has to have the last word, which has become increasingly uncomfortable for her as she's gotten older. She finds that these days she just prefers to be alone at home with her two cats and her iguana. At least they don't judge her and make her feel like an outsider and a failure.

Even outside work, family get-togethers are still a nightmare for Alison. She has tried to avoid them, to travel out of town over the obligatory Christmas family time, but everyone complains that she's "not making an effort to be a part of the family." As an adult, she doesn't have the ability to run off to play with the toys she got for Christmas when she needs a break, and watching her niece and nephew playing video games is only something she can do for a short period of time. Being around so many people all at once for such a long period of time is so difficult and exhausting. It's not that she doesn't love her family, but it's hard to appreciate them all when everyone is packed into a small area. If only there was a way to spread it out over the year and see them individually, it would feel so much better for her. To have so many people trying to talk at the same time, even if it's not to her, is hard on her sensory system as well as her ability to process what is being said and know how to respond. But she has to respond quickly, otherwise the conversation moves to something else while she is still trying to come up with an articulate response. On top of all of that, she also has to try and understand all the facial expressions and hand gestures everyone uses "to say things without saying them." That is something that has never made sense to her. If they have something to say, why can't people just say it with words instead of all these invisible gestures that are so impossible to follow and understand? It feels like trying to understand two languages at the same time. An hour is all she can take before she finds a way to make her excuses and race back to her own home, which is so quiet and peaceful. For the remainder of the day, all she can do is sit in front of the TV watching documentaries on animals while she tries to recover some of her energy to get through the rest of the day.

Neurotypicals (NT's) are social beings. They have an innate desire to seek out others and spend time with them. They seek out friends, travel around the world to maintain ties with family members, ask people to gather together for parties. They look for people they trust to be there for them to celebrate with, to comfort them, and to commiserate with them. They like to share their experiences, thoughts and ideas with like-minded people. They share their joys and their sorrows—a problem shared is a problem halved. Humans are "pack animals"—they like to be with a group. They feel vulnerable when they're alone: they feel cut off from the world around them, they can feel lonely, like no one else cares about them. They feel isolated. Spending time with other people, with friends, with work colleagues, helps NTs to feel rejuvenated, satisfied, and content. It's great to be able to catch up with their friends and hear about how their life's going, to go somewhere new, to meet new people. It helps them feel energized. It helps them feel alive.

When you ask an NT to describe a recent social interaction, they'll tell you where they went, who they met up with, what they ate or drank, and what they talked about. Rarely (if ever), do they talk about how they understood the interaction: did they engage in eye contact the whole time? How did they do this without staring and making others uncomfortable? How did they know when it was okay to interrupt and talk during the conversation? How were they able to switch between conversation topics within a single breath? How did the lines and movement of the other person's face somehow magically communicate a change in how the other person was feeling or their opinion on what had just been said. They never talk about how they do any of that. It's assumed that everyone knows how to do it—how to make a friend, how to interact with others in a way that is exciting and enjoyable instead of terrifying, confusing, and overwhelming. It's not a skill—it's just something that everyone does. You don't learn it—you just do it!

I was always really good at math in school. I could look at any problem and just know what the answer was. But my teacher would never give me the credit for getting it right because I "didn't show my working out." But I didn't see the need to—I just knew that that's the answer—what does it matter how I figured it out as long as it's right? That's what social interactions are like for me. NTs never tell me how they "work it out"—how they understand the tone of voice, the faces, how to navigate the whole conversation nightmare—they just do it. It's just not that easy for me.

Communication skills and social interactions often go hand in hand. However, if you take away the social interactions, you often don't find yourself having difficulties understanding and following the conversation. When you're alone, communication difficulties just don't exist. Why? Because when we talk or communicate with ourselves, we know exactly what we want to say, how we want to interpret it, and how to respond to it. No matter how we do it, we communicate with ourselves in a way that makes sense to us. It's simple, it's not anxiety provoking, and it's easy for us to understand.

The difficulties with communication only arise when we add another person (or other people) into the equation. We can't guarantee how other people will understand what we are trying to say, how they will interpret it, or how they respond to it. We can't guarantee that they have the same intellect or the desire to have the same level of detail for the information that we have when we are talking to them. All of these unknowns can end up being frustrating, confusing, scary, and overwhelming. These issues can be magnified even further when we're not in control of the topic being discussed, when other people contribute to the conversation, and when we don't fully understand what they are saying or why they are talking about things that are of no interest to us. And there are many, many other factors that impact our ability to feel satisfied and successful with a conversation and the communication we engage in with others.

Communication comprises many different facets: emotional and nonverbal cues are a huge piece of this. Up to 70 to 80 percent of our communication is considered to be nonverbal—the way our faces change, the emotional content of our tone of voice, the volume of our voice, the nonverbal gestures we use. All of these are integral parts of NT communication. However, these subtleties do not tend to be things that Aspies have in their communication. Being direct and specific, saying what you mean—if you don't have anything to say, you don't need to say it anyway—is often prized in Aspie communication as the most effective way to communicate. Small talk and gossip are often seen as irritating and unnecessary for female Aspies, and these often don't have a purpose for NTs other than to "enjoy" an interaction with others.

> I have a difficult time understanding the inner workings of relationships that have been made so complex (by the people engaged in them) with all of their "mind games" and similar nonsense. I have the worst case of censorship issues and usually start any new meeting with my "disclaimer"—"I am brutally honest, take it or leave it"—so if they choose to engage then it doesn't take long before they make a decision about whether they want to love me or leave me. I do not understand why people make this world and life so complicated with all of their drama.

Because of all the challenges that present with communication and the ease with which conversations and subtle cues can be misinterpreted, female Aspies can often end up feeling left out of conversations, or as if they bear the brunt of jokes for others. This can lead to the decision that it's "safer" just to be alone, because then no one can judge you, mock you, or disapprove of you. All of these negative experiences often result in difficulties in forming relationships with others, as well as in maintaining friendships with NT people.

One barrier is that the social bond-building itself seems to be widely considered more important than the stuff you talk about. In other words, the socio-emotional content of a conversation is more important than the intellectual or topical content. While I now understand that this is how things work for most people, and I can even fake it to a decent degree at times, I still do not enjoy spending much time with people where 95 percent of the interaction is bantering back and forth, small talk or conversational padding/fluff. It is exhausting and boring. But this type of talk characterizes most social chatting, so if you have a low tolerance for it, you automatically rule out most potential friends.

For female Aspies, the NT world of social interactions is a very different place. It's not that they don't want to interact with others, it's just that the experience of these interactions is very different. There are so many intricate details to any kind of social interaction that someone would only be aware of when they miss them and others don't. The effort it takes to try to understand all the nuances of a social interaction frequently ends up being more exhausting and negative than anything else. Having prolonged experiences like this often results in female Aspies feeling that it's easier to withdraw from the NT social world than to continually try to engage in it with limited (if any) positive experiences to take away from it.

> Emotionally, it's exhausting... Energy is usually taken rather than exchanged. The feeling is like being nibbled on, as if I were some kind of food source for a person who doesn't know how to get energy from the unlimited source all around us, all the time... There are very few people

whom I feel are genuinely additive to my life or my energy fields/levels.

Even though female Aspies frequently have a strong desire to engage with NTs, they often tend to withdraw from social situations, choosing to be alone and engaged in their own interests rather than with other people. The frequency of social contact (in person, by phone, text, and email) that is expected from an NT is much more than that expected by a female Aspie. The difference between these two needs can lead to difficulties, as the NT sees the lack of engagement as a lack of interest in the friendship, while the amount of engagement from an NT often leaves a female Aspie feeling exhausted and overwhelmed. Combining this with trying to stay on topic and follow what is being said (and not said!) can make relating to other people extremely difficult.

> It is difficult to relate to people. I prefer my special interests. I like some contact with people, but I struggle to find common ground in terms of "approach to life." I tend to be serious and intense and special interests driven. Most people enjoy the social realm. I find it tiring, and at times unfathomable and very strange and unnatural for me. It takes effort to talk with people about non-factual things. It physically exhausts me and I cannot absorb facial expressions, actions, and verbal utterances all at once.

Something that can make all of this even more frustrating for female Aspies is that they can also be told that their "communication style" is strange or different from NTs'. When you consider how "overly" animated NTs can be, it can often leave female Aspies questioning why their way of communicating is considered "abnormal" or socially different, while the NT communication is filled with abstract assumptions and inadvertent meaning through their nonverbal communication that can be almost impossible for an Aspie to understand without feeling completely overloaded.

> I am very technical in the way I describe things and they (NTs) find it odd. I also tend to pick up or mimic others' speech patterns. I am not aware of it until I have been doing it for some time.

One of the reasons that female Aspies tend to withdraw from social interactions with their NT peers is because NT females love to engage in social interactions that involve a huge amount of small talk and gossip. These types of verbal communication consist of a lot of emotional, subtle, and nonverbal communication that is often abstract, with their meanings being based on inferences and assumptions that result from a large variety of different facial expressions and gestures. This type of abstract communication is difficult for female Aspies to follow, as their preference is for concrete communication that is clear to understand and where inferences do not need to be made (and risk being misinterpreted).

> I would rather just be on my own sometimes than go through another pointless exercise in trying to connect, which ends in failure.

> I usually end up saying something weird, inappropriate, or stupid. It takes a lot of effort and I have a tendency to push people away after a while.

Preferring to be alone and enjoying their own company is something that female Aspies often default to in social situations because they have likely experienced a high degree of failure and rejection from their repeated attempts to interact with others. It can feel like the easier and safer option to withdraw from social interactions in order to avoid the risk of another social failure. Because of so many unsuccessful interactions in the past, females Aspies tend to anticipate that future ones will also have the same result. This can result in lowering self-confidence and self-esteem, as well as making it harder to believe in themselves. Avoidance then becomes a very effective protective factor.

> No matter how often I try and prepare and practice in social situations, the repeated failures from my past make me feel like it's more energy spent than what I can get back. I've realized over the years that it often feels easier for me to stay at home with my two cats. At least I feel appreciated and understood by them.

It's often assumed (incorrectly) that individuals with Asperger's don't understand emotions. Female Aspies certainly do understand and experience emotions—frequently they experience emotions much more acutely and intensely than NTs. In fact, females often describe themselves as being over-empathetic and feel emotions "too much." They also possess a great level of insight and willingness to describe their experiences in greater depth and detail. Women with Asperger's also find comfort and confidence in being able to practice their conversations before actually engaging in them. This practice can occur in a number of different ways, including pretend play with dolls and other props, role playing themselves and others, as well as mimicking others' personality, looks, and behaviors. Practicing social interactions and conversations in this way allows a female Aspie to identify and correct their "social errors" while hoping to end up with a script that is so well rehearsed it looks "normal" to others. Girls and teenagers also learn how to interact with others through sitcoms, movies, and soap operas. These shows allow female Aspies to practice their social skills by watching them on TV and understanding how behaviors can cause certain emotional reactions in others, as well as how other social behaviors occur within their peer group. Social behaviors, both positive and negative, are often emphasized more in these shows, which can make it easier for an Aspie female to see what is considered "appropriate" and "inappropriate" social interaction. For teenagers especially, it is important to make sure that a parent or adult is also watching with them so that they can explain that these shows will highlight intense feeling and reactions that don't typically occur within a 30-minute time frame.

There are a number of different nonverbal behaviors that can be difficult to read and understand for individuals with Asperger's. Not understanding these can have a significant impact on the ability to be successful in the social world. For example, the challenge of voice control: whether it be the volume of your voice being too loud or soft, the tone of voice being used when something is said, or whether it is related to accents that you're surrounded by. Many female Aspies find it easy to pick up the accents of others, and often do it without conscious effort, possibly as a way to try and fit in with the social group they are in at the time.

> I've done a lot of voice control over the years. As a child I had a very posh accent like my mother, which the children at my school despised. I actually learnt Irish so I could relax in a different language altogether. Then I started to speak with an Irish accent. That's gone and now I can generally moderate my accent to the situation unless I'm under stress.

As confusing as NTs can be in their communication, they can also be easily confused by the communication of female Aspies. Talking about things that are of special interest or are especially important can often be done in a very concrete and factual manner, similar to that of a professor sharing information with a class. In addition, while emotions may not be clearly portrayed in the verbal communication being shared, NTs will typically convey their emotions through facial expressions. Female Aspies can have difficulty in ensuring that the content of what they are trying to say matches up with the facial expressions that they are projecting, and that can cause further confusion for NTs:

> I talk professionally about everything and sometimes say serious things with a straight face. Sometimes my emotions do not match my facial expressions.

Engaging in communication and conversations with others, especially with NTs, can be an anxiety-provoking experience for a female Aspie who often feels such a sense of failure and frustration in these interactions. One way that female Aspies often try to manage this anxiety and fear of failure and frustration is to practice what they to say to others before they say it. This can give them a sense of control and it can also reduce anxiety over the social exchanges and interactions that can be so overwhelming and confusing.

> It gives me a sense of peace and control over a social exchange. These are for the most part quite arbitrary and stressful for me, so any preparation at least gives me some sense of preparedness and assuredness prior to the exchange. It is very difficult to explain to non-ASD people just how much effort goes into exchanges with other people.

Practicing what to say to others can result in reducing the risk of making a mistake or saying something they don't mean to. It can also help a female Aspie figure out if there are different ways that communication can happen and to keep them focused on the topic at hand.

> I can work out in my mind all possible avenues the communication could take and then figure out all of the possible responses I may need to utilize.

> I practice otherwise I am all over the place (not to me), but others can't follow my trains of thought.

Eye contact is another issue that is often difficult for many individuals on the autism spectrum. For female Aspies, engaging in eye contact is a very intimate exchange, where it can feel like someone is "looking into your soul" or is "reading your mind." It can often leave female Aspies feeling vulnerable and over-exposed to others, making them feel disconcerted and nervous.

> I feel I am invading their privacy or being too intimate.

> It seems too personal; like an invasion of their space and mine.

This is similar in many ways to how the Japanese culture sees engaging in eye contact as being very intimate and it can also be considered inappropriate with certain interactions within this culture. Female Aspies can also perceive eye contact as being a disrespectful and an overly intense behavior. To experience these types of reactions from engaging in eye contact with people you don't know intimately would of course make many social interactions feel awkward, uncomfortable, and difficult to enjoy.

It's like there is too much intensity in their eyes. I feel like they are pulling something out of me that I don't want to share. Too intimate and overwhelming.

I feel like they're trying to pull information from my soul, like they are prying and judging.

Feeling overwhelmed with the amount of information that you receive when engaging in eye contact and having to multitask by processing verbal information along with visual input from the face can often seem like too much effort, which can cause overwhelming levels of confusion and stress. By removing some of the information that results in feeling overloaded (i.e. by not looking at someone's face when engaged in a discussion or conversation), female Aspies can find it much easier to focus, process, and understand the interaction as a whole.

It's like the signal from the facial expressions interferes with the verbal signals and I have to look elsewhere to concentrate and to compose sentences and to take in words.

Reading nonverbal communication is much like the average person's experience reading a technical manual. I see the words…the question here is, what do I do with the information I see in front of me? In short, most NTs have no idea how much of their brain functions on autopilot.

Being able to look elsewhere during a social interaction and focus only on the verbal communication often helps female Aspies feel much more present and attentive to the information being given, and ultimately they are more likely to have a positive and more successful experience with the interaction as a whole. Some female Aspies also feel that their ability to engage in eye contact depends greatly on the "role" they have, whether it's in their personal or professional life.

> When I was about 15, I remember I could not look at my classmates or any other young people, not even in their general direction. My eyes would be stuck to the floor and my head would be turned away, like something outside of me was pushing it. I could not get a sound to come out of my throat. At the same time in my life, I could look straight at adults in the face and talk fluently. Now, I have a good career, which involves a lot of communication... I talk very well, I can give people difficult messages that they don't want to hear... Outside of work I feel very awkward even with the same people and although I can make eye contact it feels all wrong.

Not only can engaging in eye contact with others be difficult because it is difficult to read the faces of others, or because it provides too much information, or even because it feels like you're bearing into the soul of another, it can also be physically painful for female Aspies when they are trying to look at the faces of others. As a result, this can understandably make it difficult to follow their own train of thought or to concentrate on what's being said by others.

> The range of feeling can be actual physical pain to the feeling that by looking into my eyes, another person may attempt to absorb, co-opt, "eat" or disrespect my clarity and authenticity.

> It feels like an electric jolt goes through my ribcage. It's a very frightening feeling... It's just "too much" of the other person coming at me all at once.

Females Aspies also tend to express an awareness and understanding that engaging in eye contact is a socially appropriate behavior, and recognize that they find it difficult to moderate it in the way NTs expect:

> I engage in too much eye contact. I think people feel I stare at them.

They often feel that they can concentrate on what is being said much better when they don't have to use eye contact, depending on whom they are interacting with. If they know a person well, feel comfortable with them, and can trust them, they are likely to be able to use eye contact much more easily.

With all the nuances of social interaction, it's hard for a female Aspie to understand why NTs find social "events" so invigorating and satisfying and how NTs gain energy from them. For female Aspies, they can often be overwhelming and exhausting. There are so many uncertainties, so much effort to read the unreadable, that by the end of a relatively "brief" interaction, finding a way to recover and recharge yourself can be difficult.

> Too many emotions…too many expressions…too much going through my head at once which leads to sensory overload.

> It takes conscious effort to translate their nonverbal cues and feedback to other people in the format they want… I always have to think about everything and I get worn down very quickly.

Having to interpret all of these signals, in conjunction with hoping that you don't misinterpret what you're reading can be an extremely anxiety-provoking process for anyone. This can lead to a lot of anxiety and panic, which will only lead to increased confusion for the female Aspie, and also is more likely to produce a negative option or response from the NT who is involved in the interaction.

> I panic and get paranoid and sound grumpier and more intense than I am actually feeling. I may sound like I am yelling when in fact I am having an attack of fear and am scared, like I am lashing out. I can never be sure of others' motivations because so many people mask their uneasiness under a façade of niceness or they lie to make you feel better, and that makes me panic even more. I hate having to work so damn hard to figure out what others are thinking.

Finding a way to fit in and be accepted can also be confusing and difficult at times. Being able to do this in a way that maximizes your success can be hard. One of the many skills that female Aspies can have is the ability to observe and imitate others as a way to try and fit in.

> As a child, I was often copying other people (kids at school, storybook characters, TV characters, etc.) in the hopes that the copied behaviors would win me the approval of others. Only it didn't work, as my timing and deliverance was off. Plus there was the issue of too little or too much.

> I am a chameleon. I am an exceptional mimic and have used this to survive. It has been a survival mechanism. I also do a very good Donald Duck impersonation. I was previously diagnosed with Multiple Personality Disorder.

> A different dimension of myself—being with ordinary people is always a stage act for me. And I am an accomplished actress.

While this can help the sense of success in social interactions, it doesn't allow for the ability to be yourself, or to feel as if you are being true to the real you. Putting on an act or being a chameleon as a way to "survive" the NT social world is difficult and exhausting. It also makes it difficult for others to identify when you need space because you're having a "bad day" or for others to believe that you're not an NT. This can lead to further frustrations and difficulties as female Aspies struggle to find a way to fit in to the NT world, while still trying to find a way to be themselves.

I try to be who they want me to be.

I have done such a great job at pretending to be normal that nobody really believes I have Asperger's.

Retreating to a place where a sense of personal safety and acceptance can be felt is such an important piece of the Aspie lifestyle. This allows female Aspies to recharge, and calm down from the anxiety and panic they experience, and also allows them to review and analyze the interactions they've had.

It drains me mentally and physically. I am exhausted after having spent a lot of time with others and I need to recover in solitude.

So when relationships arise in life that can be genuine and nurturing, there can still be a lot of anxiety and uncertainty around these. The need to feel accepted by others, coupled with the fear of rejection, can be overwhelming. Like everyone, female Aspies want to trust, to love, to feel accepted, but many, many experiences in life have shown that time and time again they just end up the butt of jokes, being bullied and tormented. And then when they can find a genuine relationship that they trust and believe in, it can also cause other stresses and anxieties about not being able to have complete control over how the other person interacts with them and their environment.

> There aren't many bad things, except that they come into your house and disrupt your usual routines and drink out of the wrong glasses in the cupboard, and sometimes you just want to spend several hours ignoring them and doing something solitary or not having to be sociable. I have not yet figured out what to do about the disruption of my preferred wake-up routine, which I dislike very much. I also dislike it when our eating habits do not sufficiently overlap.

> The bad thing about being in a relationship is the fact that you are having to trust someone else that you have no control over with important things in your life, so that if they plan badly or make a mistake you have to cope with the consequences. This is a worrying thing.

The anxiety and the intensity of the uncertainty that can be experienced by a female Aspie about their desire to socialize and feel wanted, coupled with the fear of what can go wrong can lead to many negative consequences, such as self-isolation, complete withdrawal, or self-medication through the use of drugs and alcohol as a way to manage those fears and keep them "under control."

> The intensity, the emotional rawness. I have no idea how to deal with it and only dated for the first time without alcohol or dugs to help me cope with the discomfort, at age 38.

When things go wrong in relationships, there is a tendency to self-blame and look towards yourself as though you're the problem, which can be overwhelming. For a female Aspie who lives in a world of black and white, this can be a vicious, spiraling cycle that can be difficult to control. Finding a way to get these negative and often frightening emotions out of your system can be extremely important as a way to let them go and move on to another aspect of daily life.

> I will try and talk and talk and talk and write and write and write to get it out of my system. Unfortunately, that only helps so much. I tend to wallow in misery and feel like I'm a complete failure and a bad person, while being angry at the other person at the same time. It's hard to stop the torrent of negative thoughts, and it will often go on and on and on until some happier interaction comes along.

Asking for help is also something that is difficult for female Aspies, who maybe don't trust the response that they get from others, particularly if they themselves don't know what the problem is or how to fix it.

> I have found I can't necessarily trust the "help" I'm going to receive. I have felt as though I ought to be able to manage entirely on my own. I'm a perfectionist, and would sometimes rather have no help over incompetent help or sloppy help, or half-assed help. And I don't like to feel obligated—which is usually part of receiving help. I don't mind give and take; I just prefer give and take on my own terms. It's like when people help you, then you feel that they have acquired some small stake of ownership of you. *Horrible feeling.*

They also don't trust that other people will understand what they're trying to do. Aspie women often feel an obligation to return the favor, which means that they feel an obligated commitment to others that they may not want to follow through on.

> I feel I am accepting an obligation to return the favor I owe. I don't mind returning a favor except that it means that I am committing myself to meeting them again.

> Very frustrating to have others help when I am screwing up. Almost sends me over the edge when I am offered support in the middle of something I "should have" been able to do on my own.

Women can also feel that asking for help is showing other people that they have made a mistake and aren't good enough to be considered responsible or in charge of a task they have been trusted with or are expected to do. This can also result in emotional extremes that can be difficult to manage and control. As a result, withdrawal from the situation can often end up being the chosen action, even though this is often not what the female Aspie wants to do.

Managing emotions that can change at the drop of a hat can be difficult for female Aspies. Again, this is often where the need to control as much of the environment around them as possible can become extremely important in order to remain as calm and "normal looking" as possible.

> If my environment is structured then I am more stable and less emotional. I am a special education teacher in a special school. I have tremendous difficulties working in a mainstream educational setting.

With practice, some female Aspies have learnt how to control their emotions throughout the day, particularly during work (when they are most likely to be surrounded by NTs), by finding a way to remain emotionally neutral or to disconnect from their emotions as much as possible. Being able to detach from their emotions in this way can be helpful in increasing the ability of Aspie females to react in ways that can appear more "neurotypical" and try to avoid the emotional extremes that can be so difficult to control. However, there are also those times that arise when female Aspies do react to something in a way they are not sure is appropriate. This can often result in the emotional reaction becoming extreme due to the uncertainty of how others are perceiving it and how appropriate the response is.

> It is more accurate to say that I am mostly emotionally neutral, or flat; sometimes not reacting correctly to things that trigger normal people, however happy or extremely upset I am. I don't have many intermediate states and I find it almost impossible to moderate my internal emotional response. I cannot determine in the moment if my reaction is justified. Although I have an explosive temper internally, there is a disconnect between my internal reaction and my outward expression such that I need not match my outward behavior automatically to my internal reaction.

Female Aspies also tend to believe that their emotional responses can be somewhat basic, as the emotional extremes can be so visible and intense. However, during times where a female Aspie does not have the control of her environment in the way she would like, her emotional responses can become more difficult to manage.

It depends on the circumstances. If I am completely exhausted and shattered because I was up all night researching nonsense, I am a mess the next day. I am more sensitive, clumsy, etc., and less able to cope, and find myself in child-like meltdown mode.

However, when a female Aspie is focused on their area of interest or expertise, their range and control of their emotions can be quite different.

When I engage in my special interest on my own, I can access a greater emotional realm and landscape that is wonderful and safe for me, in that context.

One common misconception about female Aspies is that they do not experience or understand the emotional range of NTs, or they have an "absence" or "complete lack of emotional recognition or understanding." In fact, many female Aspies are often hypersensitive to their emotions and how others perceive their emotional responses. The difficulties they have around emotions tend to center around how to express them in moderation, without going straight to extremes. Female Aspies can be very sensitive, and as a result can worry extensively about NTs misperceiving what they are saying.

I over-feel many things, especially from other people. I'm a very passionate person and I care a lot about others. Sometimes my reactions appear too intense for some people but they just don't understand that it's because I care—maybe too much. I worry a lot about people thinking badly of me because of how I react sometimes and then I just avoid other people. This way there's less of a chance they'll think I'm a bad person and I don't have to spend the next few days beating myself up about failing yet again.

For a female Aspie, finding a way to communicate successfully and effectively with others is difficult, especially with NTs. With the anxiety of feeling unsuccessful in many social and communicative situations, and as a result being ousted from them and left to feel like someone who doesn't belong and can't follow in a conversation in the way that is expected, an Aspie can understandably experience emotional reactions that reach intense and overwhelming extremes. Finding a way to help yourself, or your Aspie daughter, to feel successful in these situations, without feeling punished by others, is key to the success of being able to develop a positive sense of self throughout life.

Living in a world of black and white can also cause difficulties in maintaining that sense of connection to others when the friend leaves our immediate environment. This can cause additional self-doubt, insecurity, and other strong negative emotions because the "NT social protocol" is made up in such a large part of unwritten and unspoken rules.

> I struggle to "feel" friendship when people are not around. I lose any sense of emotional connection and they become abstracts. It is therefore difficult to maintain relationships in a normal manner, although I have learned the fundamentals of reciprocal actions of friendship from 12-step programs (ringing people, returning calls, seeing people one on one).

The pressure to produce a social response in a quick and almost automatic fashion can be overwhelming. When responses need to be given to other Aspies, time can be taken to formulate what you want to say in the way you want to say it. There is often an unspoken understanding that "silence can be a virtue" and just because you don't respond right away doesn't mean that you're not thinking of an answer or a response to give.

> I can't command attention. When people listen to me it's clear they're just "letting me have my turn" really. Other people's conversations just wash over me because by the time I figure out what I want to respond with, the conversation has moved on.

However, within an NT interaction, the expectations are different. The expectation is that there is often a constant flow of conversation, where responses are generated, almost automatically, and the conversation changes in a fluid way that NTs understand, but never explain to an Aspie. When a female Aspie finally does provide some kind of a response, they are often told that they are wrong—they overreact or they're accused of "faking" how they really feel—because after all, Aspies just don't understand emotions! NTs presume to know what's best for them, because they think they know what's best for themselves—what other people feel, what others think. NTs are good at reading nonverbal cues, but are they really mind readers? Do they really think that it's okay to lay the blame on an Aspie for their emotional or behavioral reaction without even communicating with them, without even asking for their thoughts, or how they feel? What does an NT know about how an Aspie feels? Aspies live in a world where they feel trapped—people presume everything about them because of the label they have, or what they've done (or not done) in the past. NTs don't tend to treat Aspies like human beings with an intellect and feelings of their own. The feelings and thoughts that Aspies can identify and the communication within themselves may be done differently to how an NT would communicate their emotions, but it certainly doesn't mean that female Aspies don't experience their own emotional states.

> In general, I feel most people think in a way that's so different from mine that it's either anxiety-inducing or makes me very frustrated and makes me not want to bother. I keep feeling I say things wrong, or then I drown out more quiet individuals when I type or talk "endlessly"… I get panicky and paranoid and often feel I sound grumpier and more "intense" than I am actually feeling… I hate having to work so damn hard to try and figure out what someone is "really" thinking.

The world that female Aspies try so hard to fit into feels as though it is never going to accept them. They're always going to be an outsider, looking in, trying to fit in with people who can just barely understand and tolerate them, but NTs often leave Aspies feeling that they will never have the patience or understanding to really get to know them for who they are. The loneliness, isolation, and lack of understanding that female Aspies feel every day only causes them to withdraw even more into their own world—at least there they are safe. At least there they can feel that there is one person who can understand them. At least there, they can be "normal."

> Friends are people that share common interests, mostly. People that are similar to me and my family. People that thrive off of facts and can engage in intelligent conversation. I don't have many people in my world that I can "trust." I always found myself being walked all over and used when I opened the door to friendship.

Other times, I am misread as the "difficult, rude, indifferent one"—obviously not exactly friendship material.

SOCIAL INTERACTIONS: TOOLS AND SUPPORTS

The NT social world can be difficult to explain and understand in a way that can help a female Aspie be more successful within it. However, there are several supports that you can offer your daughter (or try yourself) to help her feel more in control and understand how to navigate the social world around her.

For children/teens

To help your daughter build her comfort and confidence with social situations, you can focus on building up her sense of feeling understood and respected. If she feels like she "isn't doing it right" or that her needs aren't being understood by you, she may withdraw from social situations and her struggles are likely to lead to more anxiety and insecurity.

With peers

Start by encouraging play dates on a regular basis with someone she feels safe and comfortable with. You want to make sure that the child you and your daughter choose for play dates is patient and supportive. Provide your daughter with specifics about the play date. Initially, you want to pick somewhere that is going to provide some structure to an activity that she can be successful at and enjoy (e.g. bowling). If she's nervous about going somewhere new, you can bring her there ahead of time so that she can see the environment and become familiar with the lighting, sounds, and smells. If there are sensory issues that are difficult for her, you can both decide if there are ways she can accommodate that (e.g. sunglasses for lights, ear plugs or headphones for noise) or if these issues are too difficult and it would be better to find somewhere else to go. You will also want to make sure she knows how long she will be there or how long the play date will last. Initially, you want to try and keep it to about an hour, so that she can feel successful, and as her confidence and comfort build, you can extend the time. It is also important to make sure she has an "out"—if things become overwhelming for her at any time, she can come to you and you can choose whether to take a walk to allow her to feel calmer again before rejoining the activity, or whether having a hug or going to the restroom for a few minutes is enough for her. Once she's able to complete the activity and interaction successfully, provide her with praise for doing so. It can also be helpful to keep a "social journal" so that you can record the success and the positive experience. This way, your daughter will have a concrete reference that she can refer to if and when she becomes anxious about her next interaction so that she can remember how successful she was last time.

Family/group gatherings

Most families have social gatherings, either with extended family or close friends, that occur on a regular basis. This can vary from getting together over the holidays, to having a regular get-together arranged with close friends. Whatever the occasion, groups of people together in a relatively confined space can be stressful and overwhelming for a girl with Asperger's. In these situations there are several things you can do to help support and encourage your daughter to feel—and be—successful.

- Encourage the host of the gathering to give your daughter a "helper" role. This could involve refilling snacks or helping out in the kitchen with food preparation. Whatever the task, it should focus on minimizing contact with too many people if that is the main source of stress for your daughter. However, if your daughter seeks out social interactions with a number of people, maybe helping out with bringing snacks around the room where she can have a defined role while interacting with others may be the most rewarding.

- Provide her with a specific amount of time you "need" to be at the gathering. This can help your daughter to know how long she has to be there. If she's enjoying herself and loses track of the time, it's okay to allow her (and you) to stay longer. Providing a time limit and an idea of who will be there gives your daughter a structure that can help her to feel more in control of the situation she is going into.

- If your daughter becomes overwhelmed during the gathering, make sure you have given her tools and supports she can use in the moment. It's important to remember that when anxiety and panic rise quickly, the logical and rational part of our brain can be difficult to access, and this is no different for your daughter. Give her one or two things (write them down for her) that she can do easily (e.g. come and find mom. If you can't find mom or dad, you can go outside and sit down under the tree at the bottom of the garden and we'll be able to find you). This allows her to feel supported by the person/people that she trusts most in the world. When she finds you, you can go somewhere quiet with her and help her calm down by going through calming techniques together.

For adults

When thinking about how to help your success when engaging with others, an important question to ask yourself is whether you want to change your behavior in social situations or whether you want to increase the acceptance and understanding of others when your differences arise. For many female Aspies, the answer is a combination of both of these options. Increasing the understanding of others of the differences you present with in social interactions and of your communication difficulties can allow for a greater sense of acceptance—why should I change my interactions when others around me don't change theirs?

Know what your limits are in relation to how many people you are comfortable interacting with—regardless of the number, be comfortable with knowing that everyone has a social limit for what they can tolerate in terms of the number of people in their space.

Be aware of when you reach your "social limit." Don't worry. Everyone has one—even most NTs! Remember that most NTs have a much greater capacity for social interactions than Aspies (they may have a bucket, while you only have a teacup). How long does it take you to reach that limit?

If you live with others, ask them to give you some quiet space when you get home from work/school. NTs will typically bombard you with questions about how your day was, and tell you all about theirs, which can lead to all kinds of off-topic extras along the way. NTs really struggle to understand that this isn't helpful for you when you come in through the door—in fact it can be so overwhelming that you may lose your temper and walk right back out of the house! Help them to understand that even having 15 to 20 minutes by yourself (maybe in front of the TV or computer checking emails or favorite websites) can be hugely helpful in resetting your system so you can be calm and more relaxed with them. Oftentimes a compromise can be to have you ask how their day was and for your NT partner (parent or room mate) to provide a short one- or two-sentence response so they feel acknowledged.

With peers

Ensure that you know where you're going with peers and who's going to be there. If you enjoy the unknown and being around new people, this may not be a priority for you, but for many Aspie females this can help them to feel less anxious and more prepared for the social event they are about to engage in.

Social gatherings

If social gatherings are something that are difficult, frustrating, or anxiety provoking for you, knowing your own limits in terms of what you can tolerate successfully is important. If getting together with a lot of people is challenging for you, or just not enjoyable, then try limiting yourself to an hour or so. Going at the beginning of the gathering can help you to get through it easier, when others are arriving.

COMMUNICATION: TOOLS AND SUPPORTS

Did your parents ever say to you, "If you don't have something purposeful to say, then don't say anything at all?" It makes sense, doesn't it? But NTs don't do this at all. They talk about everything and anything—the weather, how your day was, how you feel, day-to-day things they do—small talk that has no "purpose" other than to talk. This can often be one of the big things that makes communicating with NTs so frustrating and difficult. Add to that the need to understand all the nonverbal and "invisible" cues that NTs use to communicate too: the hand gestures, facial movements, and the constant need for eye contact—so many rules to follow. Here are a few tools that can help you or your daughter with Asperger's cope with communications with others more successfully.

• Have a list of short questions you can use to engage in brief conversation with others.

• Try and focus on a point around the face, such as the ears, chin or forehead, when engaging with others. If this is difficult or painful for you to do, try to focus on a point just behind the head of the person you're talking to. Again, if this is too difficult for you, you can just tell them that looking at their faces is too hard for you to be able to do when you're also trying to concentrate on what they're saying. Just because you're not looking at them does not mean you're not listening.

• If what the other person is saying is difficult to understand or unclear, remember that it's always okay to ask for clarification. For example, if they're telling a joke and you don't understand, it's okay to ask if they were joking. While this isn't typical in NT communication, it's much more important that you have a clear understanding of what is being said or not said so that you don't have to make assumptions and risk getting it wrong.

- If communication or the interaction becomes too difficult to continue to engage in or you're bored or it's just too overwhelming, make sure to find a way to end the conversation appropriately instead of just walking away. Walking away makes NT people think that you're being rude, which is not your intention. Find something straightforward to say like, "Will you excuse me, I need to use the bathroom" or "Excuse me I need to go and do something" and excuse yourself from the conversation in as much of an appropriate way as possible.

- Finding a way to try and understand facial expressions can be really helpful. If you have a child, start with taking photos of your own different facial expressions and have them model these. Take photos of your child's different facial expressions and the different emotions they portray. Label them and keep them in a scrapbook or journal, and have your child refer to them on a regular basis. Practice them and remember how they feel when you make them. This will help you or your child build up that muscle memory for what different expressions feel like. If you're an adult doing this yourself, looking in a mirror and taking photos of your facial expressions is a good way of helping you understand the nonverbal messages that you're conveying to others when you talk to them. It can also be helpful for you to understand what they are conveying in their faces when they are talking to you. Using these photos and the labels you give them as a reference guide can be helpful in better understanding the communication of others.

2

BULLYING

Alison has started to hate going to school. Every day she prays that she can find some way out, some way to make the torment stop. It's not torment from herself, well not entirely. It all started with three other girls. Three girls who said they would be her friends—something she has always wanted. To be a part of a group that was popular, that accepted her, that let her feel like a normal person. And they did—for a while. They would invite her over to their houses, go to the movies: they treated her like friends were supposed to treat each other. And it felt great. Moving to a new middle school, where Alison knew no one, she had felt even more alone than before. It'd taken almost a year to find these friends, a year of feeling alone in a big new school, with new classes, new teachers, new everything. One day, after coming back from spring break, Susie invited her to join her for lunch. Susie and her friends were nice—they asked about Alison and her family, what she liked, what she did over break. It was almost like a dream come true…until it changed.

After a few weeks, Susie started to make jokes—nothing too serious, just making fun of certain things that Alison did. They were small things, and Alison tried really hard to laugh it off. After all, after six years at school without friends, she didn't want to ruin this chance. She'd always been told that she tended to overreact and take things too personally anyway, so maybe this was a good opportunity to "get over it and grow up." She told herself she probably deserved it anyway. If they did something to upset her, she had probably done something to them, something to deserve it. So she worked really hard to hold it together, to laugh with Susie and her friends. But as time went by, it seemed to happen more and more, and it started to bother her more and more too. Then things started to go missing from her locker and her school bag. Alison began to notice that her new "friends" were sniggering behind her back, but not letting her in on the joke anymore. It began to feel like she was the joke. The more upset and scared she became, the more they seemed to laugh. By the end of the school year, she was glad to have the summer break to get away from them. Maybe a break and some space would help them realize that she really was a good friend.

But once seventh grade started up, the name calling and teasing started right back up with it. It was clear that no matter what Alison did, she couldn't win back the friendships that she had when the girls started being nice to her. What had gone wrong? Was it something she had done? Were they ever really her friends? It didn't take long before the name calling, teasing, and the mysterious disappearance of her belongings became much more intense. She began to get text messages from them. They would call her stupid, tell her that everyone hated her, and they would say that everyone knew she would be better off dead. She was ugly, fat, a loser—all the things that Alison would think about herself in her worst moments, and more. And it wasn't just in school anymore, it was everywhere. Her bullies could attack her no matter where she was. It wasn't like she could just leave her phone somewhere—what if her parents saw what they were saying? And she couldn't turn it off because she'd begged her parents for this phone forever. They'd only start asking questions if she suddenly stopped using it. She was trapped. Each day going to school felt worse than the last, and just when she felt that she was safe at home, the texting would start again. It was inescapable. It was relentless. It was endless. There were days when Alison had thought they were right—maybe it would be easier for everyone if she wasn't here anymore. At least it would end the unrelenting torment that consumed her day after day. Each night she would beg her mom to take her out of school and home-school her. Home-school could work for her. It would be safe; she could focus just on her work, on learning and showing her intelligence. Maybe friends were overrated after all. It could save her life.

Alison has struggled throughout her life to make meaningful connections with others. Throughout her time in school, each time she thought she met someone she could trust and call a friend, she found herself being ridiculed, being the butt of classroom jokes, or being tormented in some kind of class prank that everyone else apparently found funny, except for her. She has never felt like she has been able to really fit in, nor has she ever really felt like she has been understood or respected by anybody. Even from the supposed safety of her own home, the texting and online bullying through social media was relentless. As an adult she had hoped it would stop. She believed that people would grow up and finally stop finding enjoyment in making fun of and being mean to her. But still, Alison has had to bear the brunt of taunting at work, being picked on by her boss, and being put into situations where she feels taken advantage of and, at times, unsafe. Over the years, she has learned that other people just aren't safe for her to be around—they see her as a target and are mean and cruel in ways she can't explain or understand. The bullying she experiences as an adult seems more subtle in many ways; being blamed for other people's mistakes, people laughing about her and then becoming silent when she enters a room. Alison has never understood how other people can take satisfaction from treating her this way, and why it always seems to be her who is the target of everyone else's jokes and general mistreatment.

Alison sees others having friendships and social relationships and it seems so easy for everyone else—why does it have to feel so impossible for her? Because of her experiences, both through school and as an adult, it's extremely hard for Alison to trust others, to believe they are who they say they are, to know if they are genuine or not, to know if they really do as if her or are just trying to manipulate and use her. It feels as if it's always been this way. She has never felt accepted, understood, or a part of a group that can do things together, share secrets, feel connected to others. Because of the bullying she has survived, she feels that she can't trust anyone enough to find a true friend anymore. The idea of going somewhere new, going out with a group of new people in an attempt to develop new friendships can send her right back to the memories of sixth grade. She remembers the noises of the school, the hallway, the smells of the bullies—of their hair, their breath and the stickiness of the sweat on her own skin as she used every iota of strength within her not to fall apart in front of them. She remembers it as though she was reliving it. Every time, it still feels like it was yesterday. Her choice feels so absolute—either be alone, or risk being the target again and again. It's difficult to know how much more of the latter she can take.

It is well documented that bullying can be traumatic and leave significant emotional scars on any survivor. Repeated exposure to emotional and physical bullying can have a lifelong impact on anyone who experiences it—replaying the experiences over and over in their mind, trying to determine what they did, or didn't do, to make these situations so devastating for them. Can other people really enjoy treating others like that? For what purpose?

> For female Aspies, the tendency to hyperfocus on negative experiences causes perseveration over the interactions they had, or could have had. These are replayed over and over again—not just what was said, but the emotions that were experienced, the sensory environment, the pain, confusion, and isolation that resulted. All of this can cause erosion of self-esteem and self-confidence, which can often end up being completely destroyed. Even into adulthood, female Aspies can exhibit post-traumatic stress disorder-like symptoms when they recall experiences of bullying from their childhood. I replay it in my mind a thousand times over and over, kind of like a bad dream—what exactly did they say, how did I react, am I really like that, why am I like that, what can I change, again and again and again.

Bullying can take many different shapes and sizes. Girls can be extremely hurtful and mean to others—especially between the ages of 11 and 18. This isn't to say that people older or younger than this aren't just as vicious.

In today's world of technology, bullying comes in a variety of new forms, which can often be impossible to hide from.

Before the invention of smart phones and social media, the act of being bullied was often contained to school or the workplace. Going home was the salvation, where you were safe, at least until the next day. Today, using the various forms of social media is the newest way to torment others. Unfortunately this leaves the person being bullied in the situation where the bullying is relentless, and there are no safe places to hide. Social media has the added peril that peers can see the bullying, and coupled with the sense of safety that online anonymity can provide, the group mentality of "joining in" can oftentimes cause the bullying to escalate beyond the initial perpetrator(s), making the victim feel even more hated, targeted, alone, and unsafe.

> My cyberbullies were relentless and would never leave me alone. I wanted to kill myself because I felt there was no way to get away from them, but I was scared I'd fail because I was such a pathetic loser. I never felt safe anywhere. So I would cut myself in places that no one could see. The physical pain never matched the emotional pain I felt with what the bullies would say to me. It was only when another student saw my cuts that she asked what was happening. Then I broke down and was finally able to get help from a therapist. It all still haunts me today.

> Online friends seem to turn into bullies once they learn how pathetic I am.

Online bullying can take many different forms, from directly harassing or "flaming" the victim ("flaming" is the use of emails, instant messaging and chat rooms to harass and demean the person being bullied) to the outing of personal information in a public forum where the person can be humiliated and degraded in a number of different ways. Another common form of online bullying is through masquerading as another person. In these situations, the bully will take on an anonymous persona and impersonate a desirable relationship with the female Aspie. Once they have gained the trust of the female Aspie, the information that has been confided to the impersonated individual is then shared publicly and used to further torment, humiliate, and degrade the female Aspie. This can lead to the destruction of self-esteem and self confidence that can remain long after the bullying ends.

> I had two girls who said they were my friends who would bully me at school. Then I found a boyfriend online, and I thought it would make me normal—just like them— and then they would be nice to me. But it turned out my "boyfriend" was someone online that they had made up. The bullying became so much worse after I found out that I could hardly get out of bed in the mornings to go to school. I would beg my parents to let me stay home. Any day I did, the bullies would post things on my "My Space" and text me threats. It was impossible to get away from.

Although cyberbullying is becoming increasingly common, bullying also occurs in other ways too. Female Aspies often make easy targets for bullies for a number of different reasons. It is easy to assume that it is simply because any individual with Asperger's struggles to understand the neurotypical social world around them, which therefore makes them vulnerable. This can certainly be true—the desire to be accepted and to fit in with NT peers can be overwhelming at times. The wish to be "normal, just like everyone else" at a time when peer pressure is often at its worst can make it difficult to think about anything else.

There were times in high school when I felt that if I could just pass as normal, and be accepted by other people, then everything else wouldn't seem so hard. Most days, all I could do was focus on how I could fit in, but also how hard it was. My schoolwork suffered because of it, because I couldn't concentrate on anything that didn't feel like a possible solution to the bullying and endless loneliness I felt every day.

Bullying can also be carried out by excluding and ignoring someone. It doesn't always have to be direct aggression (whether physical or emotional) towards another person. If you've ever given, or been the recipient of, the "silent treatment" after an argument, you can understand how frustrating and isolating being ignored can be. Being ignored and ostracized from your peer group can often result in the person feeling helpless and unworthy of anyone's attention. Girls use this approach to bullying much more frequently than boys.

It was like I was invisible, like I didn't exist. Nothing I did was noticed by others. If I tried to talk to someone, they would just look through me like I wasn't even there. It left me with such a terrible feeling.

When a female Aspie feels left out or ignored by a social group, one of the things that can often be attempted is to alter her physical appearance to try and look like everyone else. This can include dying the color of her hair, trying to lose weight, and wearing the same kind of clothes as her peers. There can be many challenges with trying to adopt these techniques, which highlight the desperation for social connection and acceptance.

Starting to wear makeup can be an attempt to fit in, particular in high school. However, makeup can often feel uncomfortable, especially for girls who have sensory sensitivities.

The feel of foundation, the sensation of the powder, the dryness of the lipstick and the hardness of mascara can often make the female Aspie feel even more vulnerable, as they struggle to manage their behaviors and emotional reactions to the social isolation as well as coping with the sensory overload of all the makeup.

> I tried makeup a few times in high school. The hit on my sensory system was a nightmare and I would end up skipping the rest of the school day because I couldn't handle the sensory overload on top of everything else.

Changing the type of clothing that a female Aspie wears can also be an attempt to look like everyone else, to fit in and be accepted in the hope that they can be left alone by those who bully them. Female Aspies are often ridiculed for being different and "weird" so making the effort to try and wear the fashionable clothing everyone else does can make the female Aspie feel that they can hide in the crowd. However, oftentimes, this can cause more teasing as peers can see the visible attempts to change. In addition to this, the sensory issues that can arise with wearing certain clothing (e.g. fabric texture, seams of clothing, tags, etc.) can also increase the sensory and emotional overload, making a female Aspie feel more overwhelmed and they may find it harder to control the emotional and/or behavioral meltdown that can result.

> I tried to be just like them. I even started to dress like them (which was really uncomfortable and put me on edge all day because of my sensory issues to certain clothing). The reaction I hoped for was one of acceptance. Instead I was teased and asked, "Who do you think you are?" There was just no way to win.

I felt like they just knew how to push me over the edge. They would taunt me, poke me, and make fun of me until I just couldn't handle it anymore. Anything I tried to do to fit in just seemed to make it worse. They all seemed to delight in watching me meltdown. To be pushed to the point where I couldn't control my body or emotions anymore and to not be able to get away from the people causing it was one of the worst feelings in the world. To this day, I don't understand how people can find enjoyment in doing that to another human being.

One of the very common misconceptions of individuals with Asperger's is that they don't know how to experience emotions. However, particularly for female Aspies, most of them will tell you that it's actually the complete opposite experience. Yes, they don't tend to experience emotions in the same way that NTs do—in fact the emotions they experience are frequently much more intense and overwhelming. Many Aspies experience the world in black-or-white terms, and their emotional experiences are the same. So, in the experience of being bullied, picked on, and ostracized from their peer group, the sense of isolation, worthlessness, lack of self-esteem, and self-blame can be significantly more intense than what would be experienced by an NT. Imagine how you (as an NT) would feel being shunned and ignored by your peers, for example. Now, try to magnify this by a hundred, and you are probably closer to the experience of a female Aspie.

No one ever seemed to understand how it felt. They told me "everyone feels badly when they're left out of things," "It's not the end of the world; you can focus on other things." But for me, it was the end of the world. It wasn't that I felt "badly," it was that I felt like everyone just wanted to push me off the face of the earth—and if they did, no one would even notice I was gone. How could I focus on anything else, when this was all I could think of or feel every day?

People just walked all over me. Even the ones I thought cared about me and how I felt. They just treated me like a dirty old doormat. No one cared.

One of the things that children and teenagers are often told is that if they feel they are being bullied, then they should report it to a teacher. However, not all adults can be supportive to a child or teenager on the spectrum. They can become frustrated with the accommodations or eccentricities that are displayed daily by a female Aspie, by their stimming and pacing, their need for order, their difficulties with organization and turning in homework assignments on time, or their intense reactions when something happens out of the blue. Female Aspies can seem to make teachers feel that they "deserve it" or that they started it by irritating a peer, and the peer is just responding to the Aspie's behavior. Being told to "ignore it," or "just get on with it" are common responses that female Aspie's often report hearing when they try to tell someone they are being bullied.

My parents and teachers would always tell me to "just ignore it." But how can you ignore it when people are calling you names all day and doing things so they can laugh at you? If I told a teacher, then I was a snitch, and if I told my parents I was a "mummy's girl." If I told no one, then I felt even more alone. After a while it's just too hard not to believe you're everything they say you are.

Bullying for me was at its worst in secondary school. My bullies were merciless—they would make fun of me and tease me in the classroom— even in front of the teachers. And when I would look to the "trusted adult" in the room for help, begging them to make it stop, I found them laughing with my bullies—making it worse and making my days even more intolerable. I tried to kill myself when I was 14 years old and ended up in the hospital. It was only then that my parents finally agreed to let me do home-school. To this day, I swear it saved my life.

It can be difficult for NTs to understand what it's like to live in a world where a person doesn't have the natural ability to take the perspective of another person (also known as having theory of mind). For adults who may not have experience, knowledge, or understanding of Asperger's and how these individuals are different from their NT peers, their patience for explaining, supporting, and understanding how Aspies see and experience the world can be extremely limited, which results in the female Aspie experiencing even more stress and isolation. Long-term exposure to stress can cause many secondary issues to arise, not only in terms of the development of anxiety and depression, but also physical ailments (also known by professionals as "psychosomatic symptoms"). These can include such things as headaches, migraines, stomach aches, acid reflux, and ulcers.

Repeated experiences and exposure to bullying also result in a loss of confidence in oneself. Loss of confidence and self-esteem can also increase the risk of anxiety and depression. The anxiety that results from the trauma and loss of faith in others can also cause panic attacks at the thought of being around other people, or going into new social situations. As a result, the female Aspie can end up confining themselves to their home because it's seen as the safest place for her to be. It can limit direct exposure to bullies, although if cyberbullying is an issue, this can be as invasive as if the bullies were standing in her own living room.

Depression can also develop as a result of bullying. This can lead to not believing in oneself, which can cause difficulties in functioning at school, at home, finding a job, or engaging successfully in a career. Self-harming behaviors can also develop as a result of repeated rejection and taunting. Because the female Aspie isn't able to successfully express the emotional turmoil experienced in a way that can feel healing, engaging in self-harm can be a physical way to "see" the pain and control it. Self-harm can occur in a variety of ways, from banging her head against hard surfaces, biting herself, to physically cutting herself.

> The physical injuries I would inflict on myself were at least something I could manage. They redirected the emotional pain from the uncontrollable to the controllable.

Self-harming can lead to unintentional suicide attempts, hospitalization, and medication. While medication may be helpful in some situations, it doesn't address the root cause of why the self-injury began. It can become a highly dangerous coping mechanism and a behavior that can be very difficult to control and stop.

It's not only children and teenagers with Asperger's who experience bullying. As adults, female Aspies can also experience bullying in the workplace. The way in which the abuse is delivered can be different and is often much more subtle and harder for others to see. However, this doesn't make it any less victimizing or traumatic for the individual experiencing it. It can make it feel like it's harder to seek help and support—there is a common misconception that bullying just happens to kids. As adults, we should be able to take care of ourselves, to have the skills to stand up to others, right? Wrong!! Bullying—the act of physical and/or emotional abuse against another person—can happen to anyone at any age. The impact and devastation it can cause can be just as harmful.

> As an adult, I still find myself being bullied, but it's different to when I was growing up. It's way more subtle and passive–aggressive now, which makes it way harder to confront, or prove. I have "friends" who will randomly cancel plans we've made, or they change the plans at the last minute and don't let me know. When I call them to find out where they are, I can hear they are all together and laughing at me. It makes me feel paranoid—and it makes it even more hurtful. I decided a few months ago to stop making an effort with other people—it's never turned out well anyway.

The natural desire that female Aspies experience in wanting social relationships with others—to fit in and be accepted by their peer group—can unfortunately cause them to be taken advantage of by their peers in hurtful and cruel ways. However, it doesn't just happen between peers, it can also occur from people in positions of authority. Bosses and supervisors can also be the perpetrators of bullying. They can sense that there are staff members who are less likely to say no, to speak up for themselves, and they decide that these people can be "easy targets" for them. As adults who need a job to pay rent, bills, buy food, etc., it can leave a female Aspie feeling very stuck in a situation that they don't feel they can get out of. Leaving a job that you depend on financially can be an extremely scary (and brave) thing to do and often isn't the first option that occurs.

> As an adult, I've been bullied at work. My boss would make me take the "bad" shifts—overnights and weekends. He would threaten to fire me if I called in sick. I would be blamed for things that were clearly not my fault. I would be patronized in front of co-workers and never given any praise for the goals I achieved. Even today, five years after I left the job, the impact it had on me still causes me challenges every day.

Bullying within the workplace is often referred to as harassment or intimidation. Regardless of what it's called, it can still have a significant impact on the individual who is experiencing it. In addition, as adults, female Aspies can live alone and don't necessarily have the close physical contact and support from their parents when they walk through the door at the end of the day. Going home alone can increase the sense of isolation for adults, which in many ways can make the bullying more damaging and impactful because the tendency to perseverate and try to understand why you are being treated this way and how to stop it can last much longer when there isn't someone else there to interrupt it.

The memories and experiences of bullying are very different for an NT compared to those of a female Aspie. An NT can recall being bullied and will most often recall the bad experience and how they are glad that part of their life is over. For a female Aspie, recalling events from being bullied is often as traumatic as the actual events, even if they occurred many years ago. The female Aspie remembers the exact words, exactly how she was touched, attacked, threatened, assaulted. She remembers all the sensory information too—the smell of the environment, the people, the sweat, the fear. Every sense that experienced the bullying is recalled in the same level of detail as it was initially experienced. The distress, the ongoing nightmares, the avoidance of others or the environment(s) where the bullying occurred can be intense, often leaving the female Aspie to feel unsafe just leaving her home. As a result, they can often develop post-traumatic stress disorder (PTSD). While this isn't a common result of bullying in an NT population, it's significantly more common within the Asperger's community. It is defined as a set of chronic issues that result from long-term psychological trauma. It involves excessive fear of a specific subject or event (in the case of female Aspies, this can often be exposure to new people or social situations). As a result, the individual avoids situations that are feared and struggles to maintain any sense of safety. Someone with PTSD can also experience reliving of the events in very specific detail. This is a common thing that is reported by female Aspies who have been bullied. They can report and recall numerous sensory memories, as well as emotional and physical memories. Unfortunately, these symptoms can often go unrecognized and when the female Aspie tries to get help, the experience is often minimized with statements such as, "Well, it's over now, so you can move forward" or "What doesn't kill you makes you stronger."

BULLYING: TOOLS AND SUPPORTS
For children/teens

As a parent, you can feel so helpless when you discover that your daughter has been bullied in an environment that you send her to each day. You want her to be safe, to be happy, and to feel successful. Bullying can easily destroy all of this for her. Girls with Asperger's can sometimes have difficulty distinguishing bullying or teasing from attempts at friendship. It's important that if they ever feel that they are being treated unfairly or in a mean way by others they can tell you or another adult who they feel comfortable discussing it with.

However, there are some things that are important to do that can really help your daughter if she feels she is being bullied:

- Have an open conversation with your daughter about bullying. Let her know that if she even thinks she might be getting bullied, she can tell you right away.

- Make sure she understands that ignoring a bully does not make it go away. If anything, ignoring a bully will only make the situation worse. Bullies will often continue to escalate their behaviors towards your daughter until they get a reaction. Once they get that reaction, they will continue to use the same techniques and tactics repeatedly.

- If your daughter tells you she feels that she is being bullied, try and write down as much detail of her experiences as possible—when it happens, who is involved, what happens, where it happens, how she feels, and what (if anything) she does in response.

- Let your daughter know that it's not just other students or kids who can be bullies. Adults can be bullies too. This can include teachers, family members, and other parents.

- If your daughter has social media accounts, email or a cell phone, make sure that you have a rule that you are able to check these accounts. Make it clear that it's not because you don't trust her, but it's important for you to monitor these things to make sure that any cyberbullying can be caught as soon as possible and dealt with. This way, the bullying can stop when she gets home—her home can still be her safe haven.

- If you discover any bullying online through social media or through online games that she may play, immediately take a screenshot of the messages and then contact the administrator of the site. Inform them of the bullying and send them a copy of the screenshot to show the bullying has occurred. It is important to make sure that you request a response within five to seven business days so they can let you know how they are going to handle the situation.

- Also make sure that you are following up with any cyberbullying yourself. If it is happening through a person that your daughter knows, it is important to contact the school and also the perpetrators' parents directly to inform them of what is happening and actively work on how to resolve the problem.

If your daughter tells you she is being bullied, it's important to make sure that she doesn't feel judged or unsupported. While this is never our intention when a child tells us that something is wrong, the sensitivity and vulnerability they may be experiencing can make them hypersensitive to our tone of voice, which can cause them to feel doubted and questioned, or to feel as though they are the one at fault. It is important to work on remaining calm and asking for details of what is happening and how it is making her feel. Make sure that you identify and support her feelings around the incident(s) that she is reporting to you. When asking her about her actions or responses to potential bullying situations, it is important to assure her that you believe what she is saying and that you're not questioning whether she has done anything wrong. It is *never* okay to bully someone, and the victim of bullying isn't the person in the wrong and they haven't done anything to cause or deserve the bullying towards them.

Bullying aims to destroy confidence and self-esteem, making the person feel worthless and isolated from others. Prevention is always easier than trying to rebuild a person's confidence. Look at your daughter's talents and areas of interest and help her develop skills that she can feel proud of and confident in. Help her get involved in a hobby that she enjoys. Spending time with animals can be a great hobby, whether it's helping out at an animal shelter, working with training guide dogs or special needs animals, or taking horse riding lessons. Animals are proven to help reduce anxiety and depression in individuals on the spectrum, and having a hobby and interest that is outside school can be a huge protective factor for your daughter's confidence and self-esteem if anyone attempts to bully her.

Another skill that is important to teach your daughter is the ability to advocate for herself. Self-advocacy is understanding your own abilities and needs and the goals that you want to set for yourself. In addition, self-advocacy also involves communicating these things to others. This can certainly be a challenge for female Aspies, but work with your daughter on practicing communicating with an adult at school about things that she needs, whether they are related to assignments and schoolwork, or to difficulties with interactions with peers. It is important for her to be able to identify a trusted adult (if possible) at school, such as the school counselor or a favorite teacher, who she can talk to about more challenging issues for her. Something that you can do to help her with this is to talk with her teachers and support team at school and let them know that this is a goal you are working on. Encouraging teachers to give you updates on how she is working to advocate for herself in the classroom and school setting can also let you know that everyone is on the same page, and that she is working towards this goal. If there are difficulties that her teachers identify, they can be shared with you as they arise, which can give you a great opportunity to problem solve with her in a way that feels supportive.

Working with her to practice conversation skills with you at home is also important. To do this, it can be helpful to give her some time to decompress after school (e.g 30–60 minutes). After that time is over, set a timer for five minutes when you can talk with her about her day—you can ask her two or three questions and she can ask you two or three questions. Once the timer goes off, the conversation time is over and she can move on to do other things, such as homework. It may be helpful to try and incentivize working on this new skill in order to provide her with the motivation to participate. Over time, the time limit of the conversation can be expanded. It may be best to do this in small increments of just one minute at a time, until a timer is no longer felt to be necessary. Practicing this skill with your daughter will help her gain confidence in sharing information about her day, and will also enable her to feel more confident in approaching you about more difficult or sensitive topics that can arise for her.

If you discover that your daughter is self-harming, it's important to get her set up with a psychologist as soon as possible to work with her on the physical acts she is engaging in, as well as the emotional turmoil she is experiencing that has resulted in this behavior. While female Aspies who engage in self-harm rarely have the desire to kill themselves, this is certainly a risk that can happen as an unintentional side effect. While waiting for treatment, one thing that can help control the emotional pain that doesn't involve the risk of injuring herself in this way is to have her hold an ice-cube tightly in each hand for as long as possible. The contrast between her warm hands and the coldness of the ice can cause a pain sensation that can substitute the more dangerous behavior that she is engaging in. It is extremely important to share whatever techniques you are using, as well as the behaviors your daughter is engaging in, with a therapist who can be supportive and understanding and provide her with safe alternatives, while working with her to manage and cope with the emotional pain she is experiencing.

For adults

If you are an adult who is the victim of bullying in the workplace, there are laws that protect you. It's important to document the events and experiences you are having that are making you feel victimized and bullied. By documenting these events—the date, time, the person or people involved, what they said or did, and your reaction or response—you are building up evidence to show a pattern of mistreatment. If it is a peer or peer group that is targeting you, try to take your concerns to your boss or supervisor. It's important to make sure that this is a person whom you can trust and won't dismiss your concerns. If you don't feel safe or if you don't feel that you can be supported in doing this, then your next step is to go to human resources. Set up an appointment with them and bring your documentation and concerns to discuss with them. Regardless of whether your workplace is aware of your diagnosis, you always have a right to feel safe in your place of work. Talk with your human resources representative and make sure that any plan of action that is developed is one that you feel comfortable with. You can also contact your local disability rights advocacy network. Most countries have these available (they are easy to find by doing a quick Internet search) and will have information on how to contact them by phone or by email. These organizations are designed to protect individuals with diagnoses in the workplace and advocate for their rights and their safety.

If you are being bullied by "friends" or a peer group outside work, or within a romantic relationship, it's important to remember that people who truly care about you don't treat you in a way that continually makes you feel worthless and bad about yourself. If your friends are treating you this way, you may want to think about finding a new social group. Confronting bullies is a brave thing to do and sometimes this can help with a resolution if a person may not be aware of what they are doing and how it is impacting you. However, it can also cause the bullying to escalate if the person or people are aware of their behaviors. It is always important to remember that you are not alone. There is always help out there for you, through support groups, therapists, family members and through online forums specifically designed for individuals on the autism spectrum. No one deserves to be bullied and you haven't done anything to deserve this or cause this.

3

FOOD SELECTIVITY AND SENSORY ISSUES

Alison loves to eat certain foods—soft foods that melt in her mouth, or at least don't require much chewing. Not because she's not good at chewing things, she is, but she has found that foods that require a lot of chewing often cause the texture of the food to change—from crunchy and hard to soft and mushy, with bits of hard food getting stuck between her teeth and down by her gums. And then if there's more than one flavor, that can change too—it can become more or less intense as the texture changes. All of this together is just too much for Alison. The stress and feelings of being overwhelmed when trying to eat a meal make it easier just to avoid the wide variety of food that causes her sensory overload by only eating the soft foods, the foods that have a consistent flavor and a consistent texture. Over the years, Alison has been able to identify the foods she can find comfort with and that her sensory system can also tolerate. The color green is generally a good indicator of whether the food is going to be one she can tolerate or not. But the hardest part is that no one seems to understand why she's only comfortable eating these few foods. They keep trying to push her to try new foods—foods that overwhelm her mouth and her senses. They stop her from eating the foods that she likes, that feel safe and comforting for her. She retches when these new and complex foods touch her mouth; gags when she has to chew them before holding them in her mouth just long enough before spitting them out so that she can calm down her mouth. If only people would realize and understand that she knows what feels (and tastes) best to her; then the arguments and the meltdowns around mealtimes would just disappear.

There are other things that Alison has found herself being more sensitive to than other people seem to be. Smells are another big one for her. She knows that her teacher drinks coffee in the morning before coming to class—black with no milk or sugar. She can smell it on her breath whenever she talks to Alison in the morning. The smell is bitter and harsh and Alison finds herself backing away from her teacher when she gets too close. The smell of body sprays is one of the hardest for Alison though. When there are multiple people around her, all with different sprays and perfumes, it feels like an assault on her senses. Not only does it overpower her nose, but she feels like she can taste the smells as well. This is another reason why she hates going to crowded places, like the mall, the grocery store and especially to the movies. All the smells everywhere she goes can be so difficult to cope with and can take so much energy to keep her behaviors and emotions in control, it's exhausting.

Another thing that is hard for Alison is when people touch her. Whether it's an accidental bump in the hallway, someone putting their hands on her shoulders while she works, or—the worst of all— hugs (or "squeezes" as she likes to call them). It seems that everyone else sees these things as no big deal—the bumps in the hallways most other kids barely seem to notice—while she feels that she's being bombarded. It hurts her and it's so difficult for her to believe they aren't done on purpose. If people can see her, why can't they just move around her? All the other forms of touching feel so hard for her too. Adults keep telling her that they are all just "forms of affection and support" but to Alison it just feels like every part of her body goes into overdrive—every nerve is overactivated and begging to be released. And how long the hug or the hold is going to last can also be impossible to predict and tolerate. It makes her want to hit out just so the person will let her go and she can run away as fast as she can. How can something that makes her want to do this be a so-called form of affection?

As an adult, Alison has learned there are certain things she does that other people just don't consider "normal." When it comes to the foods she is most comfortable eating, she finds that the awkward questions she so often gets from others about the foods she eats, or doesn't eat, make it easier just to avoid eating with other people as much as possible. If she does have to go out to eat, she will spend hours pouring over the menu online to try and determine what foods she can tolerate eating without drawing too much attention to herself. It can be exhausting just to get through this process, and often leaves her with little energy left to manage the social interactions that she has to navigate during the meal. In addition to this, the smells in a restaurant, coupled with the smells from the people around her, can leave her feeling nauseated too. Too many smells hitting her senses all at once can be too difficult to cope with, especially in addition to everything else.

As an adult, Alison has tried many things to fit in with others. She so wants to have friends, to have a significant other in her life, but she never feels that she can be successful. Most social events involve loud noises, bright lights, and navigating complex and multiple conversations all at the same time. She struggles to keep up socially, while also trying to manage all the sensory overloads. As a result, she often ends up feeling ignored and left out because when she is able to contribute to a conversation, everyone else has often moved on to a different topic. The end of a night out with her NT friends, or her co-workers, often leaves her with a migraine and exhaustion that can take days to recover from in the solitude of her own home. Most social events require an element of tolerance by her senses that is just too difficult to manage for more than a few minutes. The only place where she really feels comfortable, smells and all, is at the animal sanctuary. Here, the smells help her feel safe and protected; they help her feel like she's among friends. The animals don't care if she only wants to eat green, smooth food; they don't judge her for the things that make her stand out as different everywhere else. They're just glad to see her and have her care for them.

As Alison has gotten older, she has also noticed that she's more sensitive to certain kinds of lights, mainly the large fluorescent ones in offices, grocery stores, and malls. She wears sunglasses most of the time when she knows that these lights are going to be an issue, which can certainly bring stares from others when it's dark and raining outside. But when she's with her animals, she can take them off. It feels like she's taking off her mask and can finally be herself, where she isn't judged, where she isn't asked awkward questions, and she doesn't have to endure the "hugging" that everyone else seems to see as a normal part of social interactions. With the animals, any physical contact is initiated by her; she controls it, and she knows when she can release the touch. It feels much more comfortable and natural for her. No judgment, no sensory overload, just peaceful company and unconditional acceptance.

There are several symptoms and characteristics that are common within Asperger's and autism spectrum disorder that are not mentioned in the formal diagnosis. One very common characteristic includes sensory sensitivities, which have been included in the most recent revisions of the diagnostic criteria. Sensory sensitivities can include texture issues with clothes, materials, foods, and sensitivity to light, sounds, and smells. They are often things that NTs aren't aware of and generally don't think about on a day-to-day basis, but for female Aspies these sensitivities can be so impairing that they can paralyze their system.

> I normally will refuse to touch it, but cannot convey why I refuse to touch it. I retreat a little within myself too, or try to distract myself with my iPod.

As a result of sensory sensitivities female Aspies often experience physical reactions: sweating, feeling nauseated, anxiety, and other escalations of emotions. These physical reactions can make it difficult to function in a "socially appropriate" manner, because any remaining energy that the female Aspie has is suddenly focused on coping with these negative physical reactions.

> I feel sick and I walk around in circles.

> I recoil from it. I have sometimes broken into a sweat.

Textures around clothing are an especially important issue to be aware of for female Aspies. Having a material against your skin for any period of time, let alone all day long, that is uncomfortable—itchy, scratchy, coarse, rubbing, causes pain, rashes (the list can go on and on)—can be beyond intolerable. This kind of discomfort can also impact emotions too. We all have limits to the energy we can put into anything, and once those energy stores run low, it can be difficult to manage our behaviors and our emotional responses towards others. Anyone can become short-tempered, irritable, or overwhelmed when this happens. For a female Aspie, the constant and nonstop assault on their senses leaves them feeling so hypersensitive and uncomfortable that it can cause their emotions to become easily frayed. Irritability and anger are likely to increase quickly as their energy stores are rapidly depleted. This can also lead to negative feelings about themselves, particularly for teenagers.

Teenagers can have a strong desire to wear clothing that is "in fashion" with their peers so they can look more "neurotypical" or "normal" and, they hope, fit in a little bit easier (or they may have no interest in current fashion trends whatsoever). But these clothes can be extremely uncomfortable for them, particularly if they do experience sensory sensitivities. It is at this time when the self-doubting questions can arise within themselves, such as: "Why can other people wear these and I can't?" and "What's wrong with me?" Self-confidence and self-esteem can erode because this is one more thing that seems to be easy for everyone else, yet feels so difficult and intolerable to them and is just one more issue that they feel separates them from the NT world.

As an adult I wear long sleeves and fitted jeans reasonably often because they are socially necessary but until a few years back I could not tolerate clothes that touched my skin too readily or had the wrong sleeve length and I had to have my shoes tied and retied until I could not feel them move on my feet. I still strongly prefer loose clothing and shoes that fit closely.

Touch is another sensory aspect of Asperger's that can be difficult to manage and tolerate. Touching—such has hugs, slaps on the back, tickling, high fives—that is meant by an NT as fun or jovial is often experienced by a female Aspie as overstimulating, negative, and threatening. When anyone feels threatened, it can stimulate a fight–flight–freeze response, which can result in aggression, such as hitting, kicking, punching, or biting as a way to defend themselves. Particularly when we see a female Aspie upset, an NT's natural reaction is to provide comfort, most often in the form of a hug. But for a female Aspie, a hug (or to them, a "squeeze") can be constricting, confining, uncomfortable, and overwhelming, and this leaves them feeling more upset and uncomfortable. They have no control over the pressure of the hug or the length of time it is going to last, which can both be very anxiety provoking for them. Something that can be helpful and appreciated here is to make sure that we ask an Aspie if a hug or a squeeze is something they want before giving it. This can help to reduce the risk of a panicked reaction.

> I try to get away from it (a hug), otherwise I become stressed or angry. I mostly do not like to be touched, especially lightly or in tickling. Some years back I was tickled by someone and involuntarily began shouting and kicked him in the teeth.

Food textures are also a common issue for all Aspies, male and female alike. Around 80 percent of Aspies have food selectivity issues that are related to the texture and taste of foods. For example, for an NT, eating an apple can be a very pleasant experience. It's healthy, juicy, and it tastes good. For a female Aspie with food sensitivity issues (as with a male Aspie), an apple can be overwhelming because of all the different tastes and textures it contains: the crisp skin, the soft flesh of the apple, which changes into a wet mush when chewed. The surge of juice and liquid that overwhelms the mouth, and how it all mixes together around the tongue before it is swallowed. Oftentimes it's easier just to avoid eating the apple.

At other times, foods can have textures that are craved by a female Aspie. These can be comforting and pleasurable, and can be eaten over and over again, sometimes to the exclusion of almost everything else. Foods within this repertoire may share the same texture and eliminate all others, so you may find that you, or your daughter, choose only to eat foods of a certain texture, such as crunchy foods, or soft foods.

> If it is food, I sometimes retch. Some textures make me anxious but some are comforting.

Retching is a common behavior for female Aspies with food selectivity issues. It's the body's way of getting food out of the mouth that could be potentially dangerous or poisonous. For female Aspies, retching can be an automatic reaction to try and get a food out of their mouth that is overwhelming, whether it be from the texture or the taste. When the oral sensory system is overloaded, their body's automatic reaction is to "get that thing out of my mouth" so that the senses can calm themselves down again. When we see someone retching, we often panic and worry that it's a sign that there is something wrong with the food, or that the person is choking and trying to get the food dislodged somehow. While there may not be anything "wrong" with the food in the sense that an NT means (e.g. bones in the food, it tastes like the food has gone off or is past its use by date), it may still feel or taste "wrong" to the female Aspie if it's causing their oral sensory system to go into overdrive.

There is also a rare phenomenon that can occur within a person's sensory system, where the activation of one sensory pathway can result in automatic experiences in a secondary sensory pathway. This is called synesthesia. For example, letters and numbers may be perceived as colors (known as color–graphemic synesthesia) or months and years can be seen as a 3-D map (known as number–form synesthesia). Many female Aspies have a unique ability to engage in various forms of synesthesia, which is often considered to be a "sixth sense" or "hidden sense." Utilizing this "extra" sense is something that is extremely rare for NTs. Synesthesia can occur in many forms, and appears to be a unique way for female Aspies to remember and recall a variety of information.

> If the information is written with letters or numbers, I see them in my head as colored and that is because I have synesthesia. This helps me remember things like many decimal places of pi. I remember people's smells more than anything else about them.

> I have synesthesia so I often automatically draw on synesthetic tags in order to recall something, e.g. I might remember a phone number as being green and purple or I might recall picturing something as happening on a yellow day on a particular part of my time map so I know

it was a Tuesday. A remembered sound or taste might be recalled as having a particular textural feel/visual shape (the two tend to blend) or color.

Synesthesia is the ability to perceive, experience, and interpret one sense through the perception of another. One of the more common forms of synesthesia is known as color hearing, where auditory information is experienced as certain colors. In a similar way, concrete information can also be seen with colors, and those colors can help the female Aspie to remember a variety of information and to recall that information more accurately. Synesthesia is experienced much more frequently by female Aspies than the NT population, particularly as a way to remember information or people. Another common form of synesthesia is the use of smells to trigger certain memories. Specific smells often trigger memories from the past, both positively and negatively. This is another common way for female Aspies to recall information.

> Stimuli such as smells will activate several memories associated with the stimulus—e.g. the smell of the 'muck' spread on fields through open car window will trigger memories of summer car journeys I went on as a child.

> A certain smell reminds and takes me back to an earlier time.

Information is also stored and remembered in a visual manner by female Aspies in a way that NTs typically don't experience. Being presented with information in a visual manner, as opposed to simply talking and providing verbal information tends to be a more effective way for many female Aspies to remember and store information for long periods of time. For many Aspies, the visual memory system is a much stronger method of learning, storing and recalling information than the verbal system, which is traditionally the way that NTs tend to learn, process, and share information.

> My memory works like a video so that I can "picture" in my memory where I got the information from—e.g. the page of a book or a film or where I was if I heard it on the radio.

> If someone says something, I must hear the words, understand which words are being said (I can't always do this), and then translate it into a visual meaning. When I want to speak about things it is a bit like I have to translate my thoughts from some more primitive visual medium into a written sentence, sort of memorize the sentence, and then speak it out loud. It seems that this might explain part of why I don't always understand things that I hear. I am aware that this process slows things down and that if I get stuck on trying to figure out the meaning of a particular sentence, I will miss the next several lines of conversation and get lost.

This last quote shows that there is a degree of insight into the ability to translate information from a verbal to a visual medium. While this isn't directly related to her sensory system, it does highlight the complexity of translating information from one form into another so that can it can be understood and then she is able to communicate what is going on around her. This is very common for female Aspies and can often cause delays in the ability to interact with others successfully.

Presenting information in ways that are concrete and easier for female Aspies to remember is important, not only for teaching, but also for the day-to-day information we all need to remember and recall at a moment's notice.

Teaching a female Aspie how to do this herself can be much more beneficial in the long term.

> If I really want to remember something I either have to read it several times or write it down myself. Then I form an image in my head but I wouldn't exactly call it a picture.

> I remember things best if they are written down or pictured on a piece of paper and no detail left out. I have a hard time with verbal spoken information. Then I can make up a rule or something about the information, especially a number.

Female Aspies, in the same way as male Aspies, tend to remember information better when it is presented in a visual or hands-on learning format as opposed to the more traditional verbal exchange that NTs use. The use of verbal teaching in our society is more difficult for female Aspies for many reasons. One is that the neurology of the brain (how the brain is designed and develops) for an Aspie is different from an NT, and therefore Aspies tend to remember some types of information better than other types. However, one of the main reasons that verbal teaching is generally more difficult for female Aspies to remember is because they are smothered with all the nonverbal communication that makes verbal interactions so difficult to follow and understand—the eye contact, the facial expressions, the gestures, not to mention the volume and tone of voice and the subtleties that they bring to the communication. Female Aspies can become so overwhelmed with trying to figure out what to attend to and what to ignore (a skill that tends to come much more naturally to NTs) that the essence of what is being said tends to be missed. Providing information and teaching using a visual or hands-on approach allows for patterns and visual images to be made, understood, and stored in memory in a way that is concrete and clear to the individual, making it much easier for them to recall it and use it effectively. The way in which female (and male) Aspies are able to use their sensory systems to learn, store, and process information so that they can navigate the world successfully can be very different from the way in which an NT does this. We can all be processing the same information, but in very different ways.

FOOD SELECTIVITY AND SENSORY ISSUES: TOOLS AND SUPPORTS
For children and teens
Food texture and selectivity

If you haven't already made a log or record of the foods that your daughter eats (or has eaten in the past), find out what textures and flavors she is drawn to and which ones are best to avoid. What does she tend to eat more or less of when she's happy, sad, or stressed? Or does it stay the same regardless of how she feels? Try to find a way to provide a balance of the nutrients that your daughter needs to grow and develop. If she has a very limited diet, you can use supplements—either on their own in a pill or liquid form, or in a certain food or drink, like a milkshake. It's extremely important not to try and "hide" other foods or supplements in the foods that your daughter already eats. This ultimately leads to distrust, and can cause more food refusal. Plus, with the sensitivities that your daughter has around tastes and textures, she will likely be able to tell that there is something different in her food, no matter how well you try to hide it (and don't worry, if you're a parent who's already tried this and found it hasn't worked, you aren't the first parent to try it, and you certainly won't be the last!). Allow food and mealtimes to be as honest and enjoyable as possible. Making mealtimes punishing, or shaming your daughter into trying to eat more things (e.g. "See how well your brother can eat his vegetables. Why can't you do that too?") will only lead to more food refusals, as well as lower self-esteem and self-confidence. If you are worried about ensuring she is getting enough supplements and nutrients to keep her healthy, talk with her pediatrician about it and consider seeing a nutritionist as well for further advice and recommendations. If your daughter wants to be able to eat a wider variety of foods, you should also look for a psychologist or occupational therapist who has experience with food selectivity issues for children on the autism spectrum.

It's also important to remember that when introducing or trying new foods, it is extremely rare for an individual with food or texture selectivity to try a new food and say that it's great or they want it again (if they did this, they wouldn't be nearly so selective about what they eat!). It's important to know that a new food can take up to 14 or more tries before we know for sure if we like it or not. This is often why it's important to have a professional with experience in this area working with you as you try to increase the variety of food your daughter eats.

Memory and recall

Try to work with your daughter and her school to establish ways that she learns best and help to maximize these opportunities for her. Teaching her how to make lists, or translate verbal information into a format that she can remember and recall best will help her feel successful and independent (or helping her to identify her own way to remember and recall information best), and these are also skills that will help her throughout her life. Everyone learns differently, and having a specific way that helps to maximize the way in which she learns and applies that knowledge will help her feel that her intelligence and abilities are seen by others and appreciated in the way they deserve to be. It is important to remember that finding ways to praise and acknowledge her intelligence and skills will help her develop a secure sense of confidence in herself.

Sensory issues

In regards to the texture of clothing and what your daughter wants to wear, follow her lead and don't try and push her to fit the age-appropriate social stereotypes that society has made for us all to fit into. Observe her preferences for what clothes help her to feel the most comfortable and relaxed, respect them, and teach her that it's okay to be someone who doesn't follow the same patterns as everyone else. Allow her to feel happy and confident in the choices that she makes and teach her that when she's comfortable, then her body is able to be calm and when we are calm, we are smarter (because our brain and our body aren't focused on trying to cope with all the sensory systems that are being overloaded, so then it can focus on learning and using what we know when we need it). Knowing that she has parents who believe in her and support her and, most importantly, accept her no matter what, is the most powerful gift you can give her throughout her life. Acceptance and understanding (even if we can just show that we're trying to understand) can make a huge difference to how your daughter sees herself in the world she is trying to navigate.

For adults

Food texture and selectivity

As an adult, you likely have a good idea of what foods you are comfortable eating and what foods you don't like to eat. Your preferences can be related to color, taste, or texture, and while your preferred foods may work well for you at home, where no one can judge or criticize you for what you are eating, this may become more challenging if you have to go out with others to eat, or if you want or need to change your diet (e.g. due to food intolerances, or needing to eating more fruit and vegetables). If you decide or need to increase the number of foods in your diet, for whatever reason, try not to push yourself to add in too many foods all at once. Particularly if your food selectivity is due to sensory issues, introducing too many new foods all at once can overload your sensory system, causing it to shut down and refuse any new foods at all.

Start by identifying the foods that you do like. Do they have anything in common (e.g. crunchy, smooth, same color, etc.)? If you can find a pattern, or something they all have in common, try to extend your list to include foods that might have similar properties that you would be willing to try (e.g. if you like crunchy textures and you need to include more vegetables in your diet, try putting some kale leaves in the oven. This can give them a good crunch, like a potato chip, but will also increase your intake of green vegetables). Focus on one new food at a time and try to start with only one bite. Give yourself a time limit to take the bite (e.g. five minutes) and make sure you can identify a reward for yourself once you've been able to do this successfully. Changing your diet and increasing the foods you are willing and able to eat can be difficult, not only because you are working on trying new things, but also because adopting new foods into your diet involves changing habits and routines, which can often be a challenge all by itself. Once you have been able to accept that one bite for several days in a row, try increasing it to two bites, then three. Whenever you are able to increase your ability to take five bites of the new food, you can then include it into a main meal as a small portion size. Over time, this routine will become familiar to you and to your body, and you will be able to start trying more new foods over a shorter period of time. If you find that you try a food that you really don't like, or your body reacts badly (e.g. gagging, stomach ache, or vomiting), leave that food out for now. Make a note of what it was, and what reaction you had to it and move on to something that may help you feel more successful. There will always be certain days when you can't try a new food. This can happen because of stress, distraction, or just feeling tired and not having the energy to try that day. When this happens, don't see it as a failure. Just let it be what it is—a difficult day. You can always try again tomorrow. If you find that trying to increase your diet or the foods you eat is too difficult to do by yourself, talk with your doctor about finding a psychologist or occupational therapist who may be able to help you.

Memory and recall

Everyone remembers and recalls things in their own way, and it's important to be able to identify what methods work best for you. Many Aspies are more visually based learners, so writing things down and converting things into pictures or charts can help information to be retained and also make it easier to recall later, when it is needed. Some people find that the best way they can store and remember information so it can be recalled effectively when it's needed is to file it away, like an organized filing cabinet, in their brains. If you are more of a verbal learner than a visual one, try recording yourself talking about the information you need to remember and playing it back to yourself as a way to increase your ability to store and recall it. The most important thing is to find a method that works for you and that you feel good about using on a daily basis.

Sensory issues

If you have sensory sensitivities to sound, think about finding some ear molds that you can use that can significantly reduce the decibel level of the extraneous noise around you. These can be extremely effective in reducing the noises that can feel overwhelming, while still allowing you to hear the things that you need to. If you are able to, using white noise on head phones (if your ears can tolerate them) or listening to your favorite music can also be an effective way to manage sound sensitivities at work when you are sitting at a desk.

If you have sensory sensitivities to light, you should consider wearing sunglasses, which can reduce the intensity of the sunlight your eyes pick up. Alternatively, you can also look into whether you may have something called Irlen syndrome, which can include sensitivities to bright or fluorescent lighting, slower reading speed, reduced attention, eye strain, and migraines. The Irlen® Institute provides short self-tests online to see if this may be an issue for you and if it is, you can use color-tinted lenses which will help your eyes feel more comfortable and allow you to function better by controlling and managing the sensitivities that your eyes experience every day.

For touch sensitivities, one way to help with this is to consult and work with an occupational therapist to see if there are certain techniques and therapies that may help you tolerate the necessary physical interactions that occur between people every day (e.g. handshakes, brushing past someone). Developing a short sensory routine to desensitize your body each day so that these sensations can be tolerated can be extremely helpful in reducing stress and helping your body manage the physical sensation of touch without feeling overwhelmed.

SPECIAL INTERESTS, ABILITIES, ROUTINES, AND RITUALS

Alison has always prided herself on her ability to make up and tell stories to others. Ever since she was four years old, she has loved to sit and listen to her mom tell her stories about dragons and unicorns, and all kinds of mythical creatures. If her mom didn't have time or wasn't able to tell her stories, she would curl up in her chair and read all kinds of adventure stories, where she could imagine herself as the hero who ultimately saves the day. At night, she would lie in bed and dream up her own stories with the same characters, trying to make the stories more real in her own imagination. Over the last year or so, she has started to create her own characters and her own stories, which are often quite elaborate and detailed. Her favorite thing to do is to tell her mom stories every morning when she gets up and every day after school as her mom makes dinner for everyone. The stories after school normally focus on something that has happened to her during her day—featuring characters who are the 'bad guys' and the smart yet quirky hero of the story, who is misunderstood by most, but always ends up saving the day with her intellect

and skill. Alison has the most incredible gift for someone her age to make the stories riveting and exciting, using animals as the characters in the story, primarily to disguise herself within the plot. But these stories have a deeper meaning for Alison than just finding a way to make herself feel like a hero. Not only is it a way she is learning to use to understand the social confusions of her day, but she has also found that, at least with adults, she can get the undivided attention of others, even if it's just for a short while.

Along with telling these wonderful stories, Alison also loves to illustrate her work and excels at drawing her favorite characters over and over again. Each time she draws them, she gets better at illustrating the fine detail that makes each character unique and feels like she comes one step closer to feeling that they are "perfect." Since reading the Harry Potter books, she has identified her own "patronus" (her spirit guardian)—a unicorn which she is able to draw with amazing detail in a very short period of time. This skill has also helped her to gain the approval and patience of several of her teachers at school, and, to a limited extent, her peers as well, although this attention from her peers often feels superficial and is short lived. No matter how hard she tries to use her talents to be accepted by her peer group, they never seem to be happy with her. They don't want her to draw her patronus; they want her to draw a comic strip for the school paper. But she doesn't want to use her art as comedy. For Alison, her stories and her work are serious and she wants them to be seen this way. To draw something that is outside her expertise is not something she feels confident to do— what if she tries and they want her to change it yet again. Other people just never seem to be satisfied no matter what she does.

One of the big things that Alison struggles with is whenever her routine or schedule changes at the last minute. Sometimes, people don't even tell her when there's going to be change, especially at school. Fire alarms, substitute teachers, a school assembly, a surprise test—there are so many that bother and upset her. She works hard to keep herself from showing others how upsetting and difficult these changes are, mainly because she has found herself being teased relentlessly by her peers when she does show this. To lose her ability to control herself at school is devastating and the torment she feels, not only from her peers but also from herself when she relives her meltdown later in the day, is almost too much to bear. As a result, she is frequently withdrawn and is often ignored by her peer group. But the changes in her daily schedule or routine that occur without warning or at the very last minute can be tormenting for her. Changes for her require reorganizing, re-planning, and preparing herself for the differences that will occur, regardless of what they may be. Changes in who will be interacting with her, what the expectations will be, how the behaviors of others will change, the fear of being asked to do something she doesn't know how to do. Not to mention the sensory issues of a last-minute change—the noise in the assembly room is hard on her ears and the lights are so bright they hurt. Plus there are so many more smells to deal with when there are new people around her, it just makes everything so much harder for her to manage. Not knowing when changes will happen—or 'surprises' as her teachers like to call them—can take a day or more to recover from. In a world where there is so much to misunderstand, everything has to be so carefully prepared and planned for in order to minimize the failures that can—and sometimes do—occur.

As an adult, Alison still loves to draw her characters and write her stories. Her characters almost feel like part of her family now because she's been drawing them for so many years and she feels like she knows them so well. She has found a couple of different outlets for her writing depending on her mood and what she wants to write. When she's feeling sad or overwhelmed, she has found that writing in her journal has been a great way for her to get those negative feelings out of her own mind; either through writing them down, or by writing poetry. It doesn't make the feelings disappear, but she has found that it does stop her from perseverating on them so much that she has a way to let go of them more easily. In terms of the stories she creates, she has her own website where she posts her stories and characters and generally has a good following of people who will praise her and give her positive feedback that helps her to feel appreciated. But there are always those people who seem to go out of their way to criticize her and make her feel worthless. When these people comment online, she will often stop writing her stories for a while in the fear that they will continue to criticize her work, which is something that is just too hard for her to handle. When she worries about receiving negative comments, she will share her stories with the animals that she works with. She's found that animals love to be spoken to, whether it's her talking about her day, or telling them a story. They will nuzzle up to her as she pets them, and this gives her such a sense of feeling wanted and important to them. The animals don't judge her, mock her, or insult her. They listen to her and give her affection and approval. Their acceptance and unconditional patience and love inspire Alison to learn more about them—about all animals—which she can use to add them as characters in her stories.

Now that Alison lives alone, she feels much more in control of her environment. She has the order that she's always craved—at least at home. Her cupboards have everything ordered by size, and her books, CDs, and movies are all ordered alphabetically. The order helps her feel calm; everything has its place and she knows exactly where everything is. It helps her feel more prepared for the day and knowing she can come home to the safety of her order helps her feel like she can relax at the end of the day. The difficulties still come when there are changes in her routine. Even something that is planned, like a doctor's appointment, takes a lot of organizing for her to manage and can easily throw her off for the rest of the day and sometimes longer. If there is a sudden change at work—one of her animals is sick or has to be taken to the vet—this can make the rest of the day, and sometimes the rest of the week, feel disorganized and exhausting, and things can feel more confusing than usual. It's easy for her to forget the simplest thing when something happens out of the blue. In the same way that she often struggled to be organized enough at school with turning in assignments, feeling organized enough to get paperwork done—animal training certificates, information records for the vets, things at home like taxes—can be difficult for her to do. While she loves to live in a world of order and predictability, the organizational piece of her life can be exhausting and often ends up with unwanted clutter that causes stress. When this happens, she will avoid the room that the clutter is building up in and it can often feel like it's the hidden part of her life that always seems out of control. It often has to get to an extreme before she can bring herself to try and reorganize this space. This takes a lot of energy reserves and it can take time to recover.

Not every female Aspie has a special gift, talent, or interest. But not having one doesn't make you any less Aspie. As you've probably heard many times, when you've met one person with Asperger's, you've met one person with Asperger's. As unhelpful as that statement may be at times, don't worry if you or your daughter don't have a special gift that stands out above everything else. Being yourself makes you just as unique and important. Even for Aspies who do have a strong area of interest, these can change over time, sometimes as rarely as once or twice in a lifetime, and sometimes as frequently as several times a year.

> Later in my life I became aware that I was obsessively interested in my field of work (Montessori education) and would talk ad nauseam about it to anyone and everyone and not notice their lack of interest. When I was at university I noticed my ability to focus on my pet interest—ASD— for unlimited hours in research assignments. I loved opportunities to disappear for hours on end to research my subject in the library.

Many female Aspies can choose to collect items that can either be related to a specific area of interest or have an important meaning to them. They can help a person feel calmer, connected to something important in their life, and also reflect memories of good events or experiences. The items can also carry with them sacred memories of times that they triumphed over adversity or met a challenge that brought them a unique sense of success or achievement.

> When I was a kid, I collected and categorized rocks and shells. They just seemed to speak to me and give me comfort. I loved taking care of them (I was an only child). Later I got into jewelry design and had thousands

of different kinds of beads and other findings. When I'm stressed, I like to organize my special things to feel peaceful.

I know where I got things. They are associated with special memories of places and people.

Sometimes, collections also help female Aspies focus on their dreams for the future, or can help them feel happy about their lives. When it's difficult to get confirmation and reassurance that the dreams you hold for your life are acceptable because you're so often isolated from your social peer group, having something that is concrete and tangible can often be helpful in remembering and holding on to the dreams and wishes we all have for ourselves.

I used to sometimes imagine my collectible dolls as my future children.

They are childlike and all of my animals smile (like a wall of friends that used to be a barometer for boyfriends to gauge their interest if they could stand being stared at).

When female Aspies engage with others they often find that talking about things that reflect their interests and intellect is most satisfying and rewarding for them. Small talk and gossip are often frustrating and seem irrelevant. Talking about areas of interest is a primary way to share something that you care a lot about with others. Oftentimes, however, this isn't always received with the passion and interest with which the information is offered, and it can be hard to know when people are interested, and when they lose interest.

Sometimes the people who ask me questions will start talking to someone else when I am still talking and I don't know that they are not really interested until that happens. But I think, why ask if you're not interested? This leads me at times to give an abrupt answer to the next person who asks a question about my work as I think that I won't get caught out again. Then someone like my husband will tell me that I was rude when answering—you just can't win!

Knowing when people lose interest can be difficult, and sometimes for female Aspies it's almost impossible to notice until there is an abrupt insult or action that lets them clearly know the other person is "done" with listening to them. Having to navigate this confusion and uncertainty, particularly when trying to share an area of intense interest, can be stressful and can often result in a negative experience when people ignore them or walk away. Over time, this can impact self-esteem, particularly around social interactions.

> If they are interested they will add something to the conversation or ask a question. If they are kind of squirmy in their seats and start looking around and just say something like "um" or "really" while I'm talking I know they are not interested. I do seem to talk about more things than most people that don't interest others but I am getting better at reading the signs.

> I get so excited when someone asks about what I do (I'm a genetic researcher). I apparently get carried away explaining what I do and why I love it, so people lose interest and walk away. It's soul destroying for me— to share something so important to me and have it disrespected by others. If people don't really care, I wish they just wouldn't waste my time in asking.

When the response they get from others about their interests is negative, it can often leave female Aspies feeling depressed, anxious, and confused. This can cause them to be hesitant to engage with others in the future—if I can't talk about the things that are important to me, then why am I expected to listen to other people talk about things that I don't think are important or relevant to my life? This can result in self-blame for "failing" at yet another social interaction, or it can cause withdrawal from future social opportunities in order to avoid the negative feelings that result from them. It can also result in resentment that the rules a female Aspie is expected to follow regarding the "social rules about being polite and respectful" during interactions are not reciprocated.

> I usually figure out that the people were not interested when they walk away pretty abruptly. Then, I'm like, "Crap, they aren't interested" and I go off to wallow in my own self-doubt for a few hours.

> They just get really wide-eyed. I get very worked up so I am not sure how much is my physical effect or my knowledge base. But I don't talk about my interests much anymore because then I am made fun of, even by my family.

When a female Aspie has a strong area of interest, it can become all encompassing. The hyperfocus that can arise can be so encapsulating to the female Aspie that all other things seem unimportant and are often forgotten. These can include things like forgetting to go to sleep, to eat dinner, and to greet or engage with other family members until a specific goal around that area of interest has been achieved.

> I research the hell out of everything. Once I know all there is to know about something, I am good to drop it

like a bad habit and move on. It is not until I have all the information that I need that I am able to do so. If a thought occurs to me, I feel an intense need to go search it. I get stuck in loops of researching and click, click, clicking on the Internet for most of my days.

For female Aspies, one thing that often stands out when compared to male Aspies is their interest in topics that generally arouse more compassion and self-understanding. From a biological standpoint, this may be related to how (as a generalization) females are more likely to be "genetically programmed" to be caregivers and nurturers. As a result, female Aspies may tend to gravitate towards areas of interest that focus around animals, psychology, their diagnosis, teaching, helping (e.g. nursing) and self-help. This doesn't mean that there aren't plenty of female Aspies who show interest in other areas, such as creativity, engineering, computers, and programming, etc.

I love learning about self-help, life-changing things. I'm more into factual interests...when I get a book, I read it completely to understand it and I don't stop getting books and reading them until I've fully understood the concept. If I don't have time then I won't understand it until it's completely digested.

I am a programmer and am the only woman in my department. I love my job and being "one of the guys." I avoid the gossip and negativity that I've so often experienced when I'm around other women, plus I get to do what I love. I also get to go home and be a mom, which is another one of my special interests!

Another characteristic that is common for individuals across the autism spectrum is the difficulty in coping with sudden changes in daily routines. Changes in routine can be a source of stress and anxiety, particularly if they are unexpected or sudden. However, many female Aspies find that positive changes do not provoke the same level of anxiety as other changes, although they can still evoke some nervous tension. Having a sense of control over any change that occurs tends to lessen the stress that can be associated with the unexpected.

> I am okay with changes when I am not stressed, as long as I feel that I still have some measure of control. I don't mind changes in positive situations. That noted, changes still do make me nervous. My capacity to handle change, however, is great in a positive situation.

In regards to social situations, last-minute changes to plans can be extremely anxiety provoking. Having other people join the group at the last minute, changing the location of the activity or the meeting place, or changing the time of the social event can be extremely stressful, sometimes to the point where it's too difficult to go out and engage in the social event at all. However, some female Aspies can still find the positive in last-minute changes, particularly when they involve cancelling social plans. This can be tolerated because oftentimes having time alone can be recharging to the energy that can be taken and used throughout the day.

> Cancelled appointments are usually okay because I realize that other people have schedules too, and I respect this. I hate it when people I know ask me out on short notice, though; that's very upsetting because I haven't planned for it. (This doesn't happen often, mind you—few friends— but I still hate it.)

> It depends on the change. I love it when people cancel their plans with me.

In general, the ability of a female Aspie to cope with last-minute changes depends greatly on the type of change and the emotional energy that she has. Anxiety about the unknown can also be a huge trigger to how challenging any change can be. The greater the ability to cope with this anxiety, the more tolerable unexpected changes can become.

> Unexpected changes may become quite difficult depending on my mood and my "bandwidth" to cope at the time. My whole day is a mess if there is a change under negative circumstances. This is true almost always, but not every time.

> I have learnt to cope with them a little bit better over time; they used to make a total mess of my days.

Another issue that can arise for female Aspies that can bring about similar levels of upset and anxiety is seeing other people break rules. The upset that can be experienced from this can vary, depending on the situation, the people involved, and the rule(s) being broken.

> It depends on which rules and why. It upsets me when I see others breaking rules of safety or ethics. However, I have personal rules that others need not adhere to unless they affect my property or space (eating colored candies in the correct order, categorizing or arranging things in a preferred manner).

Adhering to rules around safety and ethics appears to be particularly important for female Aspies. Rules around treating others fairly are also ones that cause a significant amount of stress when they are broken by others. This is partly because of the emotional sensitivity around bullying and the mistreatment of others, and also because many female Aspies can personally relate to the pain of being bullied and mistreated when they have tried so hard to fit in and to be accepted. The oversensitivity towards the emotions of others can also create upset when female Aspies see others being hurt (or potentially hurt) and they can react with an emotional extreme.

> We live in a time of social and emotional anarchy and wanton violence and moral corruption. Nobody seems to examine themselves much or have a moral code to live by. Very sad.

> I hate to see people treating others in an inconsiderate manner. I get mad when someone leaves their bag on the train seat while old people are standing. I get mad when parents allow their kids to do potentially dangerous things, e.g. throwing stones at passing cars or tormenting a rheumaticky old dog. I tend to tell people to act in a kinder or more responsible manner. They perceive me as interfering and tell me so.

Anxiety is very common for female Aspies for many reasons, whether it stems, for example, from challenges in the social arena, feeling different from their peers, or seeing others not following rules. There are often times when, as a way to reduce and manage feelings of stress or anxiety, certain behaviors are engaged in, sometimes in a repetitive or ritualistic manner as a way to gain control of situations that feel out of control.

> I check to see if doors are locked; pick at eyes to make sure nothing is in them; rub thumbnails smooth.

> I check that the door is locked and that the stove is turned off several times per day and especially before bed. The door checking is more of a compulsive tendency. The stove checking is related to needing to do things in steps so as to complete a task successfully.

It is not always apparent why an individual engages in behaviors they consider repetitive or obsessive. Sometimes, there isn't a clear reason that can be identified, and sometimes the reasons can vary greatly, from a way to feel a sense of control, to a way to release the build-up of emotions. Many times, the compulsive and repetitive nature of the behavior doesn't have a clear reason that the person is aware of, other than providing a sense of calm or control.

> Sometimes I need to unplug and replug something back in in different ways in a pattern so it feels right. This was worse as a child but I learned to limit these rituals to my bedroom in private. As an adult, often I can just imagine myself doing the rituals instead of doing them out in the open.

Knowing that the behavior isn't acceptable to do or discuss in front of others can bring about a lot of shame, which can inadvertently increase the need or compulsion to engage in the behavior. However, finding a way to make the behavior something that shouldn't be shamed, but can be accepted as a part of yourself can be hugely important in allowing that person to learn and use coping strategies that can help control the compulsive need to engage in the behavior. In the example above, being able to limit a repetitive behavior to a specific area (i.e. her bedroom) and also being able to imagine herself engaging in the behavior when her bedroom isn't immediately available to her is helpful in regaining a sense of control and calm.

At other times, repetitive behaviors can be adopted as a way to feel a sense of security around certain things in daily life. This can be extremely helpful, especially if there is a history of poor organizational skills, or if the person has had a negative experience due to forgetting something.

> I check and double-check things to do with numbers (I have dyscalculia, though, so I can rarely get numbers right on the first try, even with a calculator.) I double-check that important files are saved right on my computer, and make absolutely sure I have my keys with me when I leave the house.

Having a sense of security in this way around daily things can reduce a lot of the anxiety and uncertainty that female Aspies can experience, which can often drive the escalation of pent-up emotions that can result in meltdowns. Knowing that important documents are safe, or that we always have our keys so we don't lock ourselves out provides a great sense of security because we know that we haven't lost important things that we need to feel competent and successful. The reasons for repeating certain behaviors are certainly numerous and can vary significantly, whether it's for a sense of security, a need to control a compulsion, or for our own personal enjoyment. The list of reasons can be endless.

> When I listen to a particular song, I might listen to it 50 or even a hundred times before listening to something else. When I take my customary almost five-mile walk, I often listen to the same song for the entire distance, then continue on the way home. I might listen to one song for two or three days.

> Reading—I read paragraphs over and over until I understand them. I check the online dictionary for words I have not learned yet. I repeat myself in explaining things verbally to someone. I do not know why yet.

Sometimes, repetitive or compulsive behaviors can be related to a female Aspie's passion or area of interest, for example the passion to learn and continue to advance your intellect. Because intellect is something that is so highly prized by all Aspies, male and female alike, this is not an uncommon behavior that could be considered repetitive. In a world that is dominated by NT's, the subtle social cues they use automatically are things that will often be extremely difficult for a female Aspie to learn and use as easily as their NT counterparts. As a result, being able to use your intellect as a strength and a way to be seen and accepted as a successful person will continue to be an extremely important task for a female Aspie throughout her life.

> When I write something, I need to write until it is written neatly and I have written exactly what I wanted to say.

At other times, repetitive behaviors can be related to perfectionism and the belief that "if I'm going to do something, I should do it perfectly, or not at all." Handwriting can be particularly frustrating in this respect, as it cannot be guaranteed that each letter or digit will come out perfectly each time, which can result in a lot of frustration and repetitive behavior of continuing to correct work over and over again. Particularly for children and teenage girls in school, this can lead to a lot of frustrations and difficulties, which can ultimately lead to the individual falling behind in a subject, and feeling even more lost and frustrated.

> Handwriting was always so hard for me in school. If I tried to keep up with what the teacher was saying, what I wrote was illegible to everyone, including myself. If I took time to write the way I was supposed to, I became obsessed that every letter looked the same on the page—every "p" had to look the same. It was torment. Now I'm out of school, I use a computer—life's a lot easier when it comes to writing things down now.

The benefit of typing is that each time you hit a specific letter or digit, it's always going to look exactly the same, it's always going to be neat and tidy, and it's always going to be easy for any person to read what has been written. This can remove a huge amount of anxiety around this issue, so that your daughter can focus on the material and content of what is being taught instead of how tidy and perfect her handwriting is.

So whether or not you or your daughter has a special interest, gift or skill, whether there is a need to have certain routines, or engage in certain behaviors over and over again, not all of these things are required to be an "Aspie." Just like NTs, each female with Asperger's is as unique as the next, and the reasons each Aspie has for her behaviors that may seem "odd" or "different" to an NT are valid, regardless of whether they are mentioned in this chapter, or by your doctor, teacher, or therapist. The important thing to remember is to embrace your differences as part of who you are, and to learn and remember that they are what make you unique.

SPECIAL INTERESTS, ABILITIES, ROUTINES, AND RITUALS: TOOLS AND SUPPORTS
For children and teens
Special interests

If your daughter is someone who has a special interest or gift, try to help her focus on developing that skill or talent. If she likes to argue, or insists that she is always right, try and focus this in a positive way by encouraging things like joining a local debate club or team, where specific topics can be discussed, and those characteristics are prized and encouraged as they are found in the most successful debaters. If she has a wonderful imagination, or imaginary friends, look into getting her involved in a drama club and build up her acting skills, or a creative writing class so that she can write stories about what she dreams up in her imagination and can share it with others. Regardless of the talent or the interest she has, focusing on turning this into an area of confident skill and expertise will be imperative in helping her develop a strong sense of self and inner confidence that is so easy to miss out on completely as an Aspie. Encourage her to find a peer group that shares the same interests or skills, surrounding her with like-minded individuals who can support and share that interest with her.

For girls with Asperger's who don't have a special interest or gift in a specific area, it's important to help encourage them to build up confidence in the abilities that they do have. Everyone is good at something, and whether that is something big or small, building confidence in the interests and abilities your daughter does have helps her to define herself as a worthwhile individual and helps her to focus and build a sense of confidence and success as she moves forward in life. Even without a special interest or gift, NTs have shown that even they can find a way to feel successful and have fulfilling careers—if they can do it, why can't she?

Last-minute changes and routines

Catering for the need for certain routines and a sense of predictability in life is a very effective way to manage the sense of uncertainty and anxiety that your daughter may have. Anxiety is a powerful emotion, which can build up extremely quickly to become overpowering and overwhelming. Even for the person who is able to run their life on a highly predicable routine, it is impossible to completely eliminate last-minute changes. If having a sense of predictability around daily routines is something that is important for your daughter, encouraging her to learn some ways to cope with anxiety when it does start to become too intense, or a last-minute change does occur, is vital. Below are a few strategies that can be helpful:

- *Regular exercise*: This is an important part of any routine to help reduce feelings of anxiety or depression. Regular exercise helps the brain to produce chemicals called endorphins, which promote positive feelings about ourselves. Even a 15- to 20-minute brisk walk each day can be hugely helpful for this. Other forms of exercise such as swimming, Pilates, t'ai chi, or yoga can also help us to get in touch with our emotions, body, and spiritual needs.

- *Feelings scale*: Using a 1–10 scale that you develop with your daughter to identify how her anxiety or stress escalates can be a concrete and effective way to identify how intense any anxiety is and also to be able to monitor how it starts to fall as other techniques and coping strategies are used. For more information on this, you can refer to the CAT Kit, which was developed by Dr. Tony Attwood. It is also important to consult with a psychologist who has experience in working with females on the autism spectrum who experience anxiety.

- *Music*: This can be an extremely effective tool to help control and manage our mood. From classical music to instrumental, our favorite band to natural sounds in the environment, helping your daughter to identify sounds and music that make her feel calm, relaxed and in control and encouraging her to use them at times of stress and anxiety can be very useful.

- *Relaxation and visualization exercises*: Having some cards with written reminders of some deep-breathing exercises (slow deep breaths in and out), muscle relaxation exercises, or visualization exercises as ways to reduce anxiety and regain a sense of calm and control when last-minute or unexpected changes in routines occur can be helpful. It is important to emphasize that these won't cause the anxiety to disappear immediately. These are tools that need to be used over and over again in order for anxiety to start to reduce. It is also very helpful and important to make sure that any coping skills are practiced when your daughter is calm, so that muscle memory for them can be built up, making them easier to use when anxiety is heightened. You can also talk with your doctor about a psychologist they would recommend who has experience in teaching anxiety-reducing techniques to individuals on the autism spectrum.

It is important to remember that just making the suggestion of a tool or strategy is rarely enough for your daughter to start to use it as a coping skill. There is often a lot of anxiety around the idea that "if it doesn't work for me, does that mean I've failed again?" Because each person is unique, some things will work better for one person than for another. What is most important is to practice techniques when your daughter is calm. At times when she is anxious, offer to do them with her, and let her know it's okay if it doesn't work. Remind her that it will likely not work immediately. As much as anxiety can feel as if it comes on suddenly, like flicking a switch, it does not disappear nearly as quickly. Whether you are an Aspie parent or an NT parent, allow yourself to share at times when you feel anxious or stressed (e.g. stating "I feel really nervous about this meeting tomorrow. I wonder if taking some deep breaths and a bath with some music might help me calm down") so that you can model how to use these tools too. Modeling the tools and reinforcing their use are the most effective ways to help your daughter try and master them for herself.

Repetitive behaviors

If your daughter engages in repetitive behaviors, it's important not to punish or provide a consequence for the behavior or compulsion. Talk with your daughter about why the behavior and the need to repeat it is important to her, and try to understand the reason she needs to do it. Giving it a name (e.g. a sticky thought) so that you can talk about it when it comes up in a way that isn't embarrassing or shaming for your daughter can also be a helpful way to separate it from herself—a repetitive or compulsive behavior may be a part of who we are, in the way that someone may love to eat chocolate, but it doesn't define our existence, and neither should the repetitive behaviors that your daughter has. If the repetitiveness of the behavior makes it difficult for her to do other things during the day, or interferes with her ability to engage in other things, you may want to talk with a psychologist who specializes in obsessive compulsive disorder about how best to help your daughter manage the anxiety or negative feelings around the need to engage in these repetitive behaviors and the compulsions that may surround them.

Another form of repetitive behaviors, that weren't discussed in this chapter, are behaviors that are often referred to as "stimming." These can include (but certainly aren't limited to) hand flapping, spinning, jumping, making vocalizations, rubbing arms or legs, rubbing fingers together, or twirling hair. These behaviors are just as important to understand and accept as the other behaviors we have discussed, as they also serve an important function. Many female Aspies engage in stimming behaviors because they feel an intense emotion, and this is the best way for them to let it out so it doesn't become overwhelming. If the behavior causes other people to stare, talk with your daughter about how she can maybe visualize doing this behavior in public, and wait until she gets home to do it in private, or provide her with another stim that is less obvious and less likely to draw attention. The biggest concern about drawing attention is that it can further alienate her as being different. It can also increase the risk that her peers may see her as someone to bully because of a "different" behavior. It is important to remember that we all engage in stimming behavior, most of the time without even realizing it. Stimming behaviors serve an important functioning for any Aspie and the goal should never be to eliminate that behavior, but to learn to tailor it and control it so that others don't see your daughter as someone to make fun of. The more that she is able to avoid or minimize the risk of bullying, the less likely she is to experience further injury to her sense of self.

Handwriting

There are a number of different reasons that female Aspies don't like to use handwriting. Whether the reason is because of difficulties with fine motor control, muscle weakness when writing, because her writing is untidy and "imperfect," or for another reason, talk with her teachers or the school support team about allowing her to have an alternative way to take notes and respond to worksheets and test questions. In the 21st century, the majority of our work as adults is done on computers, smart phones, electronic tablets (e.g. iPad®) and other forms of electronic media, and handwriting is becoming less and less of an essential skill. If handwriting is something that is difficult for your daughter at school, look at alternatives, such as having teachers email her learning material ahead of time so she can look over it and feel more prepared. This also can be helpful because it minimizes the amount of notes she will need to take in class. When she does have to take notes, see if it's possible for her to use a tablet or a computer or laptop to type out her notes instead of handwriting them. A huge benefit to this is that she can learn to type quickly, so she doesn't fall behind in the lesson. In addition to this, each letter always looks exactly the same when the same key on the keyboard is pressed, so it eliminates the issues around perfectionism that are so often seen with handwriting.

For adults

Special interests

Special interests and skills are extremely helpful for a number of reasons. Special interests can be used as a way to refocus at the end of the day, or to calm yourself down when things feel stressful or out of control. They can also be extremely useful in determining and following a career path where you can get a sense of being valued and respected, while surrounding yourself with your area of interest, as well as other people who share the passion for your interest. Whether your interests provide a clear path to a career (e.g. computer programming, a love of numbers for accounting, self-help and learning about yourself as a start in a career to help others, such as teaching, nursing, social work, or psychology) or whether your interests feel more abstract to you (e.g. collecting stones, being an expert on dolls), you can still find a way to make connections with others who share the same or a similar interest and passion in the area that you love. If your interests don't seem to line up specifically with a career, it can be important to find a way that you can enjoy them as a hobby. Whether you do this in a solitary way, or are seeking others with a similar hobby, the Internet can be a wonderful place to find others to share your interests with. Try to remember that your special interests shouldn't be something to hide; they are a part of who you are and you should be proud of that. Whether you choose to keep your interests for yourself, or are looking to share them with others, either through hobby groups or through a career path, make sure that your choice feels right to you and isn't decided or influenced by others.

If you don't have a specific area of interest, then it's important to look at the interests you do enjoy and think about how these can be shaped into hobbies or a career path. It doesn't make you any less of an Aspie if you don't have a special interest, but it is important to find a way to enjoy the things that you care about. This is important for relaxation and as a way to reduce stress in our daily lives.

Last-minute changes and routines

As adults, we tend to have more control over our routines than children do, although it is inevitable that changes will happen that we don't like, don't expect, and aren't able to plan for. If you are someone who experiences an increase in anxiety when these things happen, then there are things that you can do to help yourself feel more in control. In addition to the suggestions that are made in the "Children and teens" section earlier in this chapter, there are some other strategies that can help. For example, keeping a folder of "unexpected changes in my schedule" can be extremely helpful. For each event that happens that disrupts your schedule, whether it's a last-minute meeting at work, or a planned trip to the doctor's, write down what the disruption was in your routine, how it made you feel on a scale of 1 to 10, if you had any negative or anxious thoughts when this change happened (and if so, what they were), what you did to calm down and feel in control again, and how long this took (see Table 4.1). Building up a reference guide like this can help you refer back to times when similar changes occurred and how you were able to handle them. It can also increase the familiarity of certain changes, and give you more confidence in your ability to stay in control of your emotions when the unexpected does happen.

Repetitive behaviors

Repetitive behaviors are important for everyone—Aspie or NT. If you have repetitive behaviors that you engage in, remember that there's nothing wrong with doing them. Sometimes they can be subtle, like flicking your fingers in your pockets, or shaking your leg to help you focus. Sometimes they can be more obvious, such as jumping, spinning, or pacing. Whatever your repetitive behaviors are, remind yourself that they are okay. They are important for us to calm ourselves, to get out emotions that are too big or overwhelming—whether through excitement or frustration or anything in between. If you have repetitive behaviors that are more obvious to others, find a private place to do them when you need to, or see if you can imagine yourself engaging in that specific behavior when you need to but aren't able to find a quiet and private place to do so. If your repetitive behavior is vocal, try recording yourself and then listening to it at times when you can't engage in it. This can help you feel some measure of relief until you are able to get to place where you can do it without being judged by NTs.

TABLE 4.1: MANAGEMENT OF FEELINGS FOR CHANGES IN ROUTINE

Date	Change in routine	Feelings (1–10)	Thoughts	Strategy	Time to calm down
9 March 2014	Emergency business meeting	Anxious – 8 Frustrated – 9	"Have I done something wrong?" "How am I supposed to get everything done now?"	Reviewed recent performance and remembered goals I've achieved Listened to my "calm down" playlist	About 1–2 hrs after meeting ended
23 September 2014	Annual doctor's visit	Anxious – 7	"What if they find something wrong?"	Took the rest of the day off work, went for a long walk, got take-out from favorite restaurant	Rest of the day – was worried about blood test results and also felt exhausted from nerves

5

GENDER LABELING

As a young child, Alison was always interested in toys that she could manipulate, toys that had a specific purpose and a clear cause and effect relationship. Her favorites were building towers with Lego® and building blocks, and playing with her brother's trucks and cars. She loved banging them into each other—the noise the blocks made compared with the Lego®, the spinning of the wheels on the cars—and opening and closing the doors over and over again. They did exactly the same thing every time she played with them and the rhythmic pattern in which the wheels of the cars spun or the doors opened and closed in the same way was almost soothing for her. She knew what to expect when she picked the toys up, she knew they would do the same thing each time.

But the adults around her didn't seem to like her playing with her brother's toys. Her parents, relatives, and her teacher always seemed to want her to play with "normal girl toys." They would give her dolls and ponies and tell her to "go and play nicely with the other girls." Alternatively, she was told to go and pretend to be a fairy princess who is rescued by a prince on a big white horse. But these toys and games didn't serve a purpose for her—she didn't enjoy playing with them, or pretending to feed a baby or carry it around. And trying to engage in pretend play with others just seemed mystifying to her. How do you even pretend to be someone else? What's wrong with being yourself, and why does some prince need to rescue her anyway? How do you figure out what to do if you're pretending, not only to be someone else, but someone who isn't really real in the first place? Where's the fun in that?

What was even more confusing to her was that other girls her age seemed to love doing these things. Watching them play these pretend games seemed so confusing to Alison, trying to follow a storyline at the same time as navigating the complex social rules that were so intimately intertwined in the stories. How did these girls know what the plan was they had to follow? And how was she supposed to fit in and follow this secret plan too? Why couldn't people just leave her alone to play with her cars? Not only did people give her a difficult time about the toys she played with as a young child, but when she finally did begin to play with dolls, she was told she was "too old" to play with Barbie®. People were never happy. But she never played the pretend games that other girls seemed to. She used her dolls to try and understand the social interactions she'd experienced that day and especially to try and figure out places where she'd made some kind of mistake. If only she could figure out her social error in the interaction(s) that had occurred that day, then maybe she could come up with a solution so it wouldn't have to happen again.

As if being told she couldn't play with the "right toys in the right way" wasn't hard enough, Alison was also pressured to wear what she would call "girly clothes": clothes that were made of more than one type of material, which was hard on her skin and difficult for her sensory system to process and tolerate; clothes that were brightly colored, and sometimes multiple bright colors that hurt her eyes and gave her a headache; clothes with frills and lace and itchy things; clothes that were tight on her body with seams that felt like they were digging into her until all she wanted to do was to rip them off. Boy's clothes were so much more comfortable—they were baggy, easy to find in dark colors that her eyes could tolerate. Yes they had tags (which she could take off) and seams, but the looseness of the clothing on her made the seams feel as though they weren't there—she could tolerate them easily. The fleecy material was soft and comfortable to wear, not itchy and painful. Why did people care what she wore so much anyway—surely if she was comfortable, that was the most important thing? Couldn't they see that when she was comfortable in her clothing, she was calmer and her days were more productive and more successful? Why was it that everything she wanted to do always seemed like it was the wrong choice to everyone else's?

As an adult, Alison had hoped that the issues around her "gender neutral" clothing would disappear—adults can make their own decisions, right? People will respect those decisions and won't question or argue with you about them, right? Wrong! Even as an adult, her parents continue to nag her about her baggy, dull clothes. Why can't she dress more like a woman, why can't she get her hair done, why won't she wear makeup when she goes out? How is she ever going to fit in and find herself a husband to settle down with? Alison has always struggled with the concept that what she wears and what she puts on her face will determine who will like her, who will accept her, and who will be able to "put up with her" for the rest of her life. Why does it all have to be so superficial?

Nothing Alison has ever done or worn has made her feel like she can fit in with everyone else, and on the times that she's tried, she's felt so uncomfortable and her body has felt so overwhelmed that those days have been horrendous for her to get through. As for getting her hair cut, going to a hair stylist is a nightmare—to have someone she barely knows stand so close to her, touch her, and engage in pointless small talk for so long. It's uncomfortable and stressful and she can't wait to get out of the chair and race back home. Plus the smell of the products they use—from the smoothing gel to the hairspray—leaves her feeling nauseated for the rest of the day. Alison has found that having long hair is relatively easy to manage on her own—it's easy to trim and she can just pull it back into a ponytail or put it up in a bun if she needs to. Plus she's able to avoid all the awkward small talk and uncomfortable touching and smells. Who cares if she has had the same hairstyle for 20 years? She's learned how to tolerate and manage this area of her life with as little stress as possible and even the idea of changing this feels overwhelming to her.

Dressing in a feminine and socially acceptable way is something that has never gone well for Alison. People tell her she's attractive, but when she wears the clothes that everyone else wants her to and puts on makeup, she's noticed that people pay much more attention to her. While having more social connections is something that Alison has always wanted for herself, the attention she gets when she dresses the way everyone else wants her to isn't about making friends. It's mainly from NT males, who flirt with her, make comments that she doesn't know how to respond to and she finds it difficult to get away from these situations. As confusing as most social interactions can become for her, the addition of sexual interest and flirtation is even harder and more uncomfortable for her to cope with, especially when it's not expected and is from people whom she barely knows. After having these kinds of experiences multiple times, and feeling such sensory overload by the end of the day from the clothing and the makeup, Alison has made the firm decision that looking "pretty and feminine" is just not worth it. Being comfortable within herself is what matters the most to her. She just can't figure out how to make other people understand that.

The gender labeling within our society—from toys, to clothes, to the social expectations of how we present ourselves to others—can be another set of almost unspoken, but very visible social expectations that at times can dominate how we judge or accept others. As with many aspects of life, female Aspies can vary widely in their preferences for many things. For many girls with Asperger's, it's not necessarily the interest in the toy that may seem different, but the intensity of the interest, or the way it's played with.

I played with dolls every day until I was 14 years old.

It's often considered "unusual" for a girl to play with dolls past a certain age, but for many girls with Asperger's, the familiarity of their toys, the way they play with them (e.g. acting out social situations to better understand them) or the meaning the toys hold can lead female Aspies to continue playing with them for much longer than is typical of other girls their age. For other female Aspies, the idea of playing with feminine toys at all seems like a foreign concept.

I was given dolls, but never liked to play with them. I preferred my brother's toy trucks and cars.

I hated girls' toys. I liked stuffed animals and plastic dinosaurs. I also liked baseball and plastic army men and Roman soldiers. I liked robots too.

Many stereotypical girls activities were stupid, boring, and inexplicable.

Many female Aspies report that, as children, they tended to play with toys that made them "tomboys." This may be because of social differences in engaging with boys and engaging with girls—boys are generally more literal and direct, and easier to understand socially, particularly at a younger age, whereas NT girls tend to be much more complex; they want to play with dolls, make up stories, and create imaginary worlds to play in. They can use much more subtle ways of communicating and interacting than their male counterparts. In general, they place greater emphasis on the emotionality of a situation and their thoughts and opinions of people or characters involved in their play. It can be extremely difficult for a girl with Asperger's to pick up on and understand these "rules" around who a character is, how they are feeling and why, and what other characters think of them. Male toys are more concrete and black and white—you play with cars, you have a car chase. You play with trains, you act out an episode from *Thomas the Tank Engine*. The subtleties of emotions and opinions are much less likely to be involved in this kind of play, which can feel much more comfortable for the female Aspie.

Boys are more logical.

Sometimes I played with boys' toys because a younger boy was willing to play with me. I did not have friends my own age, only younger children or adults.

I was given "gender specific" toys such as Barbie® dolls but I did not play with them the same way that all the other girls I knew played with them. The other girls wanted to play out getting married scenarios whereas I played out adventure scenarios such as replacing Tarzan with my Barbie® as the hero rescuing my brother's Action Man® in the jungle.

Many other female Aspies tend to prefer to play with gender-neutral toys and activities, mainly because there is a specific purpose and functionality to the toys they choose. This feels like a much "safer" choice instead of risking engaging in imaginative play, which can be much more unpredictable, harder to follow the rules of, and can feel so difficult to maneuver through, especially when you have enough challenges in navigating the real social world. Playing with gender-neutral toys provides a sense of purpose to the activity in a more concrete way, such as creating buildings with Lego®, without having to risk making an error or not understanding the "rules" of creative play. Especially for children, if they are expected to play in a game where the social rules are unpredictable and rapidly changing, the rules can seem very difficult and confusing to follow. As a result, any child will likely lose interest in that activity and go in search of one that is more enjoyable to them and easier to understand and feel successful with.

It is more accurate to say that I am gender neutral. As a child I liked to play with boys because I enjoyed toy cars, Lego®, building blocks, sports, and that kind of thing, and sadly girls are not often given toys like cars and blocks;

also girls were more complicated, and unkind in ways I didn't understand.

I loved playing with Lego® for years and had many thousands as a child. I also loved cardboard boxes, and drawing/writing. I always ignored the dolls I was given.

Are model aircraft considered "toys?" Is there a gender attached to them? I preferred nature or animals to toys.

Just as many female Aspies can identify themselves as enjoying or preferring gender-neutral toys; gender neutrality can also be a prevalent issue with clothes. Clothing preferences tend to combine comfort and texture as their primary issues of importance, and many girls or women with Asperger's tend to prefer either wearing "girl-only" clothes (skirts, dresses) or gender-neutral clothing.

I wore and wear jeans and shirts and most of my clothing is gender neutral. I generally don't like dresses or skirts and find many of them impractical, too ornamental, and uncomfortable; likewise women's dress shoes. I usually wear unisex sneakers or brown loafer shoes. Although I am an adult I bought my first-ever long dress and pair of heeled shoes to wear to a wedding this year. I am told that I began refusing frilly clothing and dresses by age one and a half.

Most of the time I just need to be comfortable. I just wear what I like no matter what the fashion or place or whatever.

I like to wear either old baggy pants or skirts. I love to dress in my ballet outfit and I have a few fairy "outfits."

For many female Aspies, the fashion of the clothes is significantly less important than the comfort of wearing them throughout the day. Being able to feel comfortable in what you are wearing allows for your energy and attention to be focused on the social and emotional aspects of any day. In turn, this increases your ability to focus on tasks, complete them successfully, and not feel burnt out or overwhelmed by sensory and texture issues of uncomfortable clothing. While there are also many girls on the spectrum who love to wear "girly" clothes and fashion, these individuals don't tend to struggle with the sensory overload that can be so challenging and physically draining to a female Aspie who has to navigate this issue in addition to all the others within her day.

Sometimes the preference to dress in a gender-neutral manner is simply because a female Aspie doesn't identify with feeling either masculine or feminine, and so they dislike the expectation that they have to fit into a certain category in order to be identified. Similarly, makeup, which is very much a social expectation for NT females, can often have sensory issues associated with it that make it uncomfortable to wear.

I can't stand the feel of foundation on my skin, and eye makeup stings my eyes. I do wear lipstick a lot.

Makeup is greasy and disgusting, especially lipstick.

The decision to wear makeup doesn't always have to be a sensory issue; sometimes it can be a personal preference. Many female Aspies have an awareness that NTs can treat them differently based on how they look on the surface.

I hated dressing as a girl and still resent the makeup but I do it now, and well, because people treat me better if I do.

As an adult I am more likely to choose shirts and jeans that are cut for women instead of men because I realize that this is socially expected, but my clothing is otherwise gender neutral.

Trying to find a way to feel more socially accepted is often something that female, and male, Aspies try to achieve through whatever means they can (up to a point). While female Aspies can understand that the social world is something they won't completely master in the way NTs do, being treated in ways that allow you to feel more accepted by peers can have a huge impact on any person. For a female Aspie, being able to remember a positive social experience based on a change that they made to their physical appearance can help them to feel that they may have some control over their social world and environment. As uncomfortable as it may be to dress in a "socially stereotypical" manner, the pay-off of feeling more accepted by others may outweigh the discomfort of wearing makeup or clothes that are considered to be in the "current trend." Female Aspies can have a profound memory for details that NTs typically miss or overlook. Whether the detail is focused around how to feel more accepted by others, or whether it is related to other issues and areas of their life, this is a skill that can be a special strength for many. Having this eye and attention for detail can make Aspies extremely talented in careers that are typically defined as more male dominated.

I enjoy engineering and computer programming, which is unusual for a woman, even now.

I am an engineer, a male-dominated profession. I like motorbikes and mechanical things. I find it much easier to communicate with men than with other women.

Having the attention to detail and the ability to hyperfocus on preferred areas of interest makes areas such as engineering, computer programming and accounting perfect careers for many female Aspies. Although this is not exclusive to all female Aspies, these types of jobs can provide a lot of satisfaction because they have limited interaction with others and are also very concrete in what they require. For example, computer programming requires specific code in order to develop a program that works efficiently, so the input and development has to be precise and exact. There is little to no room for error or assumptions or approximations. Because the work is specific and exact, it can work well for an Aspie mind.

Another area where gender can be an issue for female Aspies is around their own identity. Female Aspies can consider themselves to be more gender neutral as opposed to identifying themselves as either male or female in their preferences. This is different from their sexual orientation, which is based on physical and sexual attraction towards others. Gender identity is a person's sense of their own gender and it is a subjective experience, as opposed to one defined by physical characteristics. There are many factors that can play a role in the development of gender identity. Female Aspies who consider themselves as gender neutral or don't identify as predominately male or female define themselves based on their interests and intellectual traits more often that NTs. While there are many possible reasons for feeling this way regarding a person's own identity, expecting such individuals to conform and fit into a specific "gender box" can often result in them experiencing lower self-esteem and confidence, particularly as they transition into adulthood.

I do not see myself as particularly female or male; I have many male and female interests and behaviors, I am not good at treating people "as women" or "as men" and I dislike the current trend of placing a psychological distance between men and women; I don't really understand why certain things are for women, other things are for men. To me, humans are humans, men only marginally more understandable than women, and I am just me.

I am generally not interested in appearing particularly feminine or masculine because I don't identify with either.

There can be many potential challenges with not feeling connected or not identifying with the biological gender you are assigned at birth. Having a gender identity that is different from your biological identity can cause a lot of confusion, especially based on the reactions and expectations of others. This can significantly impact self-esteem and self-confidence. Our society, and most societies around the world, strongly emphasize the "importance" of gender identity and expect these assumptions and expectations to be in line with our physical characteristics. For female Aspies who feel that they may have more of a male or neutral identity, this can lead to confusion from peers, unfair judgments, name calling and other difficulties. On top of the other challenges that female Aspies may experience, this can further impact issues related to anxiety and depression, making the ability to feel accepted by peers even more challenging.

GENDER LABELING: TOOLS AND SUPPORTS
For children and teens

If you notice that your daughter is showing a preference for toys and interests that are considered to be more for boys than for girls, try not to change this for her. Encourage her to explore and develop her natural interests and curiosities and give her praise and encouragement for doing so. What matters is that she has a passion and an interest in what she is doing, whether that's playing with Lego® and trucks or learning about game design and computer programming. Trying to push her to have interests in more "gender appropriate" toys and interests risks her feeling confused about what she wants, and giving her the sense that what she is naturally drawn to is wrong in some way. Encouraging her to be who she wants through supporting her interests, her choices in clothing, and how she perceives herself in terms of her own gender identity will give her a lifelong strength that will stay with her and help her through more challenging times in her life.

In regards to the clothing your daughter chooses to wear, remember that what's important is her personal comfort. If she can feel comfortable in what she wears, she will be able to focus better at school or in a job, and be more productive, giving herself a greater sense of confidence and success. The more she can feel confident and secure in herself, the more she will be able to stand up to those who misunderstand her in the world around her. Regardless of whether her clothes are more male or female in their preference, try and respect her choices, and understand that her decisions are most likely being made on how comfortable she feels in them, as opposed to what they look like to everyone else.

At the end of the day, we can't control how the world treats our children, but we can prepare them as best we can. The more you can help your daughter to feel supported and accepted by you, regardless of how she dresses or what her interests are, the more you will give her a sense of confidence in herself that will serve as the biggest protective factor as she moves forward in her life. Acceptance and understanding (even if we can just show that we're trying to understand) can make a huge difference to how your daughter sees herself in the world she is trying to navigate. The biggest gift you can give your child is the ability to believe in herself and to know that you, as her parents, believe in her too.

For adults

The toys, interests, and hobbies that we have as adults are often seen as more acceptable to others, regardless of whether they are male or female focused. Interests and hobbies that tend to be more mechanical, focused on transport, building or numbers, or more physical in nature tend to be considered more "male-focused" interests, while interests and hobbies that are more focused on caring, art, or cookery tend to be considered more "female focused." Regardless of where your interests lie, embrace what you care about. Hobbies help us relax and enjoy our free time. They help us to decompress from the stresses of our everyday life and focus on something that we enjoy, and help us to feel good about ourselves. Finding out what that is for you is a very individual process. Regardless of what other people think of them, and whether they're "more for guys" or not, your interests, passions, and what you enjoy are for you, not necessarily for others, unless you choose to share them.

When it comes to the clothing that you wear, regardless of whether you prefer to dress in feminine clothing, neutral clothing, or what society defines as masculine clothing, make sure you wear what is comfortable for you, and appropriate to the environment you are in. If you have sensitivities to seams of clothing or specific textures, make sure that you avoid these. Having to cope with an overloaded sensory system on top of the everyday stresses we all encounter can send you into sensory overload, where you have no energy at the end of the day to be able to recover well. Also, be aware that certain social situations (e.g. a wedding) may have an expectation of wearing something more feminine. If this is the case, and it is something you need to attend, you can choose to wear a dress, or alternatively, look for something in a material and style that is more suitable for you (e.g. a smart pant/trouser suit). What is most important is that you are able to feel comfortable and confident in the clothes you are wearing for the majority of the day, particularly in social situations, where there will be other unexpected pressures that occur that you likely don't have control over, but nonetheless still have to deal with successfully.

At the end of the day, you are who you are—you are unique and special in this world and have a lot to offer. Embrace your interests and preferences, whether they be in the clothes that you wear, or the hobbies you enjoy. They are what make you, you.

6

PUBERTY AND MENOPAUSE

Alison has always felt like she struggles in so many areas of her life. From getting other kids at school to play with her, trying to figure out how to avoid being teased and bullied by others, having to learn how to tolerate clothes that cause her sensory system to go into overdrive, to finding people who are interested in what she's interested in and are willing to allow her to participate in that interest with them. Even as a younger child, she never felt like she really fitted in, and as she gets older she notices that the differences between her and her peers seem to grow more and more. While she feels like she's getting used to this, it's just the way it's always been and probably always will be.

But recently things have changed. Just when she thinks things can't get any worse, they do. But it's different this time. Her emotions are suddenly so much harder to control. Emotional meltdowns seem to be happening a lot faster and more often for no apparent reason. They feel harder to control, harder for her to calm down from, and they happen at the most random times. Alison has had emotional meltdowns before, typically when things she doesn't expect happen, or when she experiences social or sensory overload. She has always worked hard to hold it together in school and save those meltdowns for the safety of her own home, but every day it seems like it's becoming more difficult and more exhausting to do this. Not knowing when the emotional overload is going to hit her, not knowing when something she used to be able to handle just fine might send her into a panic or give her a sense of overwhelming frustration. Shutting down in school seems to be the only way not to draw attention to herself —to go to her "happy place" as her mom calls it, where she can focus on her stories, her characters, and her artwork. She is doodling more in class and as a result she's not paying attention to the teachers, which results in its own set of problems. She's not ignoring them because she doesn't care or doesn't respect them. It's a survival tool at this point. Ignoring everything around her and focusing on her interests so she can get through the day may cause her to get into trouble and fall behind in classes, but at least she's able to manage her emotions and behaviors, at least while she's at school. When she goes home, she can fall apart, in the privacy of her own bedroom (if she can make it up there fast enough). She just wants to be alone when she feels this way. To have other people become frustrated, angry, scared, or disappointed in her because of behaviors she can't even control anymore only makes her feel worse and more worthless than ever before.

Another thing that isn't helping her anxiety are the changes in her body. Since starting her period, she's also developed breasts, pubic hair, and shapely hips. All of these changes seemed to happen so quickly. She has learned about growing up and the changes that come with it from her parents, through numerous books and from classes in school, and has never looked forward to it. When things change, she wants to feel that she has some control over them, and now she has none. Her world feels like it's been taken over by someone else, and she has no say in anything anymore. Even at school, amidst the bullying and teasing, she sees that boys are starting to give her more attention. But she doesn't trust it anymore—is it genuine attention, or are they just setting her up for more teasing? Not that she's interested in boys anyway. But all of her female peers seem interested, so it's hard to know how to cope with this. It just feels like one extra thing to add to the stresses of her school day. On top of all this, she now has to wear a bra everyday, which feels tortuous, itchy and generally just uncomfortable. But even worse than this is when she gets her period and has to use sanitary pads. This feels so unnatural and uncomfortable and she dreads it more every single month. No one else seems to understand how she's feeling. She's just told, "Now you're becoming a woman and this is what everyone does." It's supposed to feel like some sort of proud "right of passage" in life, but to Alison, it just feels painful, uncomfortable, and one more thing in her life that is completely out of her control.

With all of these changes in her life and her body, coupled with the meltdowns and the fear she experiences with them and feels no control over, she will often try and hold it all in until she goes home. Once she gets home, it all comes out— the fear, the anxiety, and the anger. Her parents have told her that she will scream, shout, bang her head or her fists against the wall, and scratch herself on her arms and legs until she bleeds, but most of the time she's not even aware of what she's doing because her emotions are so overwhelming in those moments. She has also noticed calluses developing on her fingers from biting herself in classes to try and control her behavior at times when she can't "allow" herself to explode. As if life wasn't bad enough before, now it feels like all of these changes are permanent—she has no control over anything anymore. Will she ever be able to have control over herself again?

As an adult, Alison has gone through many challenges in her life and, for the most part, she now feels like she's in a good place in her life—she has a job that helps her focus on her areas of interest, she's found a way to live her life in a way that is peaceful for her and provides her with the social interactions that she needs while also giving her her own space and privacy to decompress, relax, and recover from days that are more stressful.

At the age of 43, things have started to change again. She has begun to have periods of anxiety for no apparent reason, her sleep seems more irregular than usual, and she is struggling more with negative thoughts, which she felt she had under control for quite a while now. All of this seems to be happening at the same time as some other changes—her periods are now irregular, they are more painful, and they leave her utterly exhausted. After talking to her doctor, she realizes that she's starting menopause—or perimenopause as it's technically called. It's almost like being thrown back in time to when she was 12 years old and she first started getting her periods. While she feels she has more tools and experience to handle it now than she did back then, nonetheless she still feels miserable. If she survived this entire nightmare once before, why does she have to go through it again? The night sweats and hot flushes are hard to cope with too. Waking up with her sensory system in overdrive because she is lying in a bed covered in sweat is stressful, uncomfortable, and generally just feels nasty. She worries all the time about how these changes, and the impact they're having on her mood and her energy levels, might be affecting her job and her ability to interact with others. She fears that these changes, which are once again completely out of her control, may cause her to lose the few relationships she has, and possibly even her job. Without her job, how will she pay her mortgage, buy food, pay her bills? The worry and anxiety keep spiraling and it feels as if there is no way to stop them. The tools she has learned in the past—how to replace these thoughts with more rational ones, how to relax, how to focus on calming her body—just don't seem to be working anymore. All of these negative thoughts feel so rational and her fears seem so genuine and real in the moment. What if she really does end up losing everything that she has spent her life working so hard to build up?

PUBERTY

Puberty is something that everyone goes through at some point in their late childhood or adolescence. Male or female, Aspie or NT, it's unavoidable. For girls, they typically start puberty around the ages of 10 to 12 years and finish between the ages of 15 to 18 years. Hormones go haywire, causing emotional sensitivity, mood swings, arguments, and an increasing desire for independence. For a female Aspie, however, this can be very different. Without even considering the impact of hormonal changes, the physical changes that occur for girls as they go through puberty can be overwhelming for the female Aspie. The lack of control, the lack of predictability, and the fact that they have no choice regarding the changes that are occurring can be enough to cause emotional overloading. The one thing that female Aspies, for the most part, have been able to keep control over is their own body—what they wear, how they look, what they eat, how their hair is cut. Suddenly, their whole body starts to change in ways that are visible, not only to themselves but to others. Many girls on the autism spectrum often feel that socially they are behind their peers, so the onset of puberty often happens before they are ready for it. As a result, they may try any way they can to control and minimize the changes. Unfortunately, when this happens the one thing they can control is their food intake.

> All I cared about was making sure my body didn't change, or at least controlling how it changed. I remember reading that being underweight can stop your period. It consumed every waking moment for me for years. I would write out lists of foods along with their fat content and calories. I had no idea I had an eating disorder until the doctor told me I had to stay in the hospital because I had anorexia.

> I was told my anorexia was caused by "psychological issues." I was anxious and depressed. Of course I was! I was put on a planet I didn't belong on, where no one understood me and where I suddenly started to lose control of my emotions and my body. I had to take the control back! The thin people in my school looked happy, they were popular, and they looked like they didn't have a care in the world. I wanted that more than anything.

Limiting food and controlling weight can also delay the development of breasts, and females can often feel that they can retain their "childlike" body image. This reinforces the need for control, and so the cycle of restricting food intake is reinforced and continues. Feeling that you have some form of control over these changes can also limit the attention that is received from boys at school. While many female Aspies desperately want to be accepted, the idea of a romantic or sexual relationship can seem very overwhelming. There are so many aspects to a romantic or sexual relationship (e.g. holding hands, kissing, physical intimacy, understanding another person's emotions, etc.), that it can feel like too many things to manage all at once, from both an emotional and sensory perspective.

The hormonal changes that occur during puberty can also impact the emotional and sensory systems of a female Aspie. The sensory sensitivities to clothing and the need to use bras and sanitary pads can significantly increase sensory overload and subsequent meltdowns. The development of body odor and the need for showers can also be huge issues for female Aspies.

It wasn't just the scratchy discomfort of a sanitary pad, it was the sticky, smelly blood that I had to deal with too. It hurt too. Stomach pains and back pains for a week every month sent my meltdowns into overdrive. It was just too much to handle all at once.

I hated showers—the feel of the water, the smell of the soap and shampoo. Plus there's just too many steps involved.

On an emotional level, it is generally understood that teenagers can become moody, irrational, and argumentative. However, for a female Aspie, emotional changes feel much more unpredictable, uncontrolled, and significantly more intense than they have done before. Anxiety and depression can easily feel more prevalent and more dominating in everyday thinking, making it difficult to focus on anything else. As a result, relationships can suffer—any friendships at school, as well as relationships at home with parents and siblings. Schoolwork can also be impacted. Suddenly not getting the grades that you've been able to get before can increase the sense of anxiety—the "what ifs" that can dominate thinking, primarily about your own abilities and personal sense of value. In addition, the negative thoughts that can result from these things can also impact self-esteem and self-confidence.

Around the age of 13, my anxiety went though the roof. This meant it was harder to control (or be aware of) my stimming. My parents also told me that I became much more rigid and controlling in practically every aspect of my life.

Social rules became so much more complex. It was as if everyone else had taken a class in them (social interactions) without inviting me.

The more anxious I became, the more obsessive I got. It was all I could do to try and control my world, which now seemed so out of control.

The anxiety that may be experienced during puberty can often go hand in hand with depression. When self-esteem drops significantly and the world around you feels so out of control, self-harming behaviors can develop, most commonly as a way to punish yourself or to find a physical outlet for the pain and confusion that are trapped inside. From a biological standpoint, physical pain to the body causes the release of endorphins, which can help the person gain a pleasurable sensation. When you feel overwhelmed with depression, anxiety and low self-esteem, being able to control a pleasurable rush can be very powerful. Self-harming behaviors can come in many forms and can include cutting, biting, head banging, burning, and scratching, among others.

I hurt myself when I'm angry or frustrated at myself. The scars are a constant reminder of how useless I feel.

They make me feel more worthless, which makes me hurt myself more.

I started cutting myself when I was about 15. It wasn't just to punish myself, I also found it comforting. It helped me match my outside self to my inner self when I didn't know what else to do.

Self-harming behaviors are often used as an outlet for emotions that can't be expressed verbally, and therefore cause a sense of loss of control. They are considered easy or automatic to engage in because they are initiated by the person and can be done at any time. While people who engage in self-harming behaviors often state that they feel a release or reduction in the emotional turmoil they experience, they also report that these behaviors can be very difficult to stop later in life. It is important to work on helping your daughter recognize that what she is going through, while it is difficult and may feel like it will never stop, will eventually start to feel better and that there are safer and healthier ways to cope than to inflict physical harm on herself. As impossible as it may seem, there is light at the end of the puberty tunnel for everyone.

MENOPAUSE

In the same way that puberty isn't easy for the female Aspie or those around them, menopause can cause very similar stresses, both physically and emotionally. Perimenopause occurs first and can last several years. It is characterized by irregular periods, which can become either heavier or lighter, longer or shorter in duration. It typically starts around your mid 40s to late 50s. During this time, women can feel exhausted, irritable, have hot flashes, night sweats and increased emotional difficulties. Female Aspies often experience increased physical pain around menstruation as well as an increase in, or onset of, migraines.

It's like being a teenager again, but now I have so much more to lose.

As with puberty, mood changes can be intense and sudden, and it can be difficult to predict when they might occur. In addition to the increase in anxiety and panic attacks, an increase in anger can also occur. Because of the irregularity of periods during this time, it is difficult to predict when your period may occur. Again, this causes a sense of loss of control. Having a sense of losing control can cause an increase in anxiety, frustration, and panic at any age for a female Aspie. However, around the time of perimenopause or menopause, the sensation of losing control is increased even more due to changing hormone levels which make the emotional overloads much more intense and difficult to manage. As a result, phobias and obsessive behaviors that might have been an issue in the past may reoccur.

I hate the craziness of my cycles. One might be 12 days; the next cycle might be 50. It makes it impossible to plan anything.

Trying to cope with all of these symptoms at the same time can be exhausting in itself. It takes a lot of emotional strength and energy to be able to manage on a daily basis. This becomes significantly more difficult when perimenopause starts to impact your energy levels as well. Lethargy and exhaustion are also common symptoms of perimenopause. When a female Aspie doesn't have enough energy to get through the day, it causes difficulties in her ability to find the energy for emotional regulation, dealing with the pain of menstruation, hot flashes, and the sensory issues that go along with all of this. With all of this to cope with at the same time, it's not surprising that female Aspies can be left feeling overwhelmed. The difficulties in engaging with others in the way that they used to can also cause difficulties in their social relationships—at work, with their children, partners or friends. Having additional challenges in social relationships, on top of everything else, can also increase the sense of personal failure and worthlessness, leading to the occurrence (or reoccurrence) of depression. Depressive symptoms can also spike in their intensity around the time of ovulation.

> I know when I'm ovulating because I get so depressed so suddenly. When this happens, everything I've learned just evaporates.

> I am grumpy, short tempered, and quicker to yell at my husband and my kids. As a result, I feel like my entire family tries to avoid me, which make me feel even more of a failure. It all just feeds the guilt and the depression.

Being overwhelmed, whether it be emotionally, physically, or from a sensory overload, can cause the brain to forget the tools that have been used to manage symptoms in the past. This can increase the feelings of exhaustion as well as feelings of failure too. Negative feelings tend to spiral in a way that can make everything feel out of control and too difficult to cope with anymore. All this, along with the physical pain of cramping and joint pain, can make the ability to think logically and be able to function in a way that is expected impossible at times.

> I just can't think right anymore. I get angry for no reason but I can't make myself stop. Everyone tells me to "stay strong," but I'm so tired I don't know if I can anymore.

Hot flashes can also be challenging during perimenopause and menopause. Feeling hot suddenly for no apparent reason can cause the sensory system to easily feel overwhelmed and can also induce a feeling of claustrophobia, where the body reacts in a "fight, flight, or freeze" response.

> It feels like the heat is suffocating me and I can't get away from it.

Hot flashes at night (also known as night sweats) can also have a significant impact on a female Aspie. Waking up feeling as though you are sweating the way you do when you have a fever and realizing you are lying in a bed of sweat can not only cause sleep difficulties, but can also result in the "icky" feeling that sweat can leave on your skin until you are able to take a shower.

> I wake up in a pool of sweat and have to change my PJs and lie on a towel. The slimy feeling on my skin doesn't go away until I'm able to have a shower, which sometimes I have to do two or three times a night.

As difficult as it can be to feel this way when you are trying to get rest and sleep in order to be able to cope with the following day, disruptions in sleep can also impact mood swings, loss of energy, and depression. It can feel like the symptoms of menopause are exacerbated and can cause an even greater sense of feeling overwhelmed. For many women who are on the autism spectrum, having "survived" puberty only to have to re-experience similar symptoms during menopause can feel as though they can never "catch a break" or never be fully in control of the emotional and physical sensations within their own bodies.

PUBERTY: TOOLS AND SUPPORTS
For children/teens

One of the most difficult things about puberty is that it happens to everyone, so there's nothing we can do to avoid it. While puberty is normal for all teenage girls, your daughter's experience may be very different because she is on the autism spectrum. The emotional turmoil can be much more intense and can make her feel much more confused and out of control. If she is struggling with this, consult her doctor about how to help her. Birth control and other medications for anxiety and depression may help stabilize some of the emotional irregularity, which can help your daughter, but it can also make her feel worse. If this is something you want to try, make sure you monitor her moods carefully, and encourage her to do the same. While it can take several months for birth control and other medications to stabilize, side effects can include an increase in low mood and a lack of energy. If you are concerned that it is making her feel worse, make sure you share your concerns with her doctor. Remember, it's important never to try any medications or supplements without first consulting with your daughter's doctor.

Other strategies that can help your daughter include making sure that she has a healthy diet and plenty of daily exercise. Even taking a 20-minute walk after school while listening to music on an iPod® or other MP3 player can dramatically help her to decompress from her school day and regulate herself before starting on homework. If she is open to it, try and encourage her to keep a journal about her feelings and experiences. Whether this is done in a traditional journal, using an app on a smart phone, or through dictation software, such as that produced by Dragon®, this can be a great way to process emotions and experiences and can be a much healthier way to cope with the changes that occur during puberty. Alternatives to keeping a journal also include writing stories, poetry or song lyrics as other outlets for her emotions.

If you find that your daughter is experiencing emotional highs and lows that are difficult to predict and are causing her distress, a good technique to help her is to visually track her moods to see if they correlate with menstruation and ovulation. Tracking this together can help her see any patterns that may arise throughout the month, so that over time she can start to predict when she may have days that are going to be more emotionally challenging for her and can learn how to better prepare for these and increase her self-care around these times. It can also be useful for you as her parent, and for the rest of the family, so that you can see when she may need more space or more understanding than usual.

Providing her with the opportunity to work with a therapist or a psychologist can also help her learn how to identify and cope better with the changes and challenges that arise during puberty. Sometimes, having a person to talk with who is outside the family and school environment can help her feel safer in discussing things that are difficult for any teenager to discuss. For many individuals on the autism spectrum, most people have defined roles in their life, so having a professional who has the role of teaching skills and helping with emotions and behaviors could be very important and effective for your daughter. It is important to make sure that any professional that she works with is familiar with working with teenagers on the autism spectrum so they can be aware of the different experiences that occur for your daughter, compared with her NT peers.

If you are concerned that your daughter may be engaging in self-harm behaviors, it's extremely important to talk with her doctor or therapist immediately. Make sure that when you talk with your daughter about it you are able to be calm and convey your support and love for her, so that she doesn't feel shamed or embarrassed by the discovery of the behavior. Help her to find other ways to express her emotions that don't physically hurt her, and always make sure you consult with a professional about how best to help in these times. Also, if you can, try to keep a log of any new injuries or episodes you discover or witness, so that you can share these with her doctor and/or therapist.

MENOPAUSE: TOOLS AND SUPPORTS
For adults

Because of the lack of research into adults on the autism spectrum, it can be extremely difficult to find research to show how life changes, such as menopause, impact the quality of life of a female Aspie and their ability to manage their emotions and physical symptoms in addition to everything else in their day-to-day life. While this can lead to difficulties in finding a therapist or someone who can understand that what you are going through is different from an NT woman, it doesn't mean that you can't find help and support if you need it. Talking to other women with Asperger's and getting their experiences and perspectives can not only be helpful in giving you anecdotal support that you can then share with your doctor or medical provider, but it can also be extremely empowering for you personally to know that you're not the only person going through this. Looking into online forums on Aspie-friendly websites and blogs can be a great place to start.

In addition to mental health support, there are also supplements and medications that can be helpful in reducing the symptoms of perimenopause. While there is a lot of information online on different vitamins, medications, hormone creams, and other herbal remedies that can be useful, it is always important to consult with your doctor before starting any medication or supplement regime to make sure it is the best option for you and doesn't interfere with any other treatments or medications you are taking.

Dietary changes can also be helpful in managing symptoms of menopause and perimenopause. Reducing high-fat and high-sugar foods and increasing fruit and vegetables are commonly recommended changes. However, as with most dietary changes, different changes help different people so it's important to talk with your doctor or dietician first.

Exercise can also be an important thing to adopt in your daily routine. Starting an exercise class or going to the gym can involve increased social pressure, which can be difficult when you're already coping with a lack of energy and emotional overloads. If this seems like too much for you, try a solitary activity, such as brisk walking for 20 to 30 minutes a day. Exercise is proven to improve mood and reduce anxiety in addition to other physical health benefits. While nothing can remove the symptoms of menopause and perimenopause, making the right lifestyle changes can improve your daily symptoms.

7

CLOSING CHAPTER

Girls and women on the autism spectrum are unique in many ways. The way in which they present their symptoms and challenges is significantly different from males on the spectrum, which has been a long-standing issue with the lack of diagnosis and misdiagnosis of so many girls and women around the world.

Within the social world, female Aspies often hide themselves much better than males. They are fundamentally different from their male counterparts because they often have a more innate desire for social connections and relationships. They tend to be observers of others as a way to try and fit in with their peers. They watch what others are doing and try to understand the social rules as opposed to either jumping in and trying to control interactions, or deciding to ignore them completely. Ignoring social opportunities for female Aspies often results from repeated attempts at joining others, which are continually met with rejection. It often ends up seeming safer to avoid the attempts than to try and feel the sense of failure again. Because female Aspies engage in more passive behaviors when they feel socially overwhelmed, such as withdrawing, becoming quiet, or avoiding eye contact and social interactions with others, adults often see these girls as "shy and cute" as opposed to being concerned that something else might be causing the withdrawal. This is one common reason why so many girls are overlooked for a possible diagnosis. Because of a female Aspie's desire to be accepted by her peers, coupled with her difficulties in understanding many of the nonverbal social nuances that are used by neurotypical peers, bullying is not uncommon and can cause significant stress and depression when it goes unidentified and untreated.

Females on the autism spectrum can also experience a number of sensory issues in their day-to-day lives. Sensitivities related to touch, taste, texture, noise, smell, and food can cause a female Aspie to consume a significant amount of energy just trying to get through the day. Trying to tolerate these sensory overloads can feel like these sensitivities are almost constantly assaulting her sensory system. If you or your daughter experience sensory sensitivities, make sure you can identify exactly what the sensitivities relate to and then you can develop strategies to cope with and manage them.

Emotional extremes are also common in female Aspies. While female Aspies work hard to hide these in public (i.e. at school or at work), they do happen most often in the safety of their own home. Emotions, like most things for females on the autism spectrum, are experienced in "black and white," which means that female Aspies often feel either calm, or extremely upset, or frustrated. It can be difficult for them to identify triggers and sensations in their body that can lead to the emotional extremes they experience. These emotional extremes and meltdowns often occur because they are exhausted, have been coping with a social or sensory overload, or are going through hormonal changes that are associated with puberty or menopause.

When these happen, work with your daughter to calm her down and get past the meltdown. Once your daughter is calm you can talk with her in a much more productive way about what happened and why these behaviors occurred. When any of us experiences significant emotions, whether we are on the autism spectrum or not, our brains struggle to process verbal instructions effectively, so helping someone become calm before starting that conversation will have more beneficial results. Whether this discussion happens through visual aides (e.g. drawing out situations, writing things down in notes or via email or text, or talking) find what works best for your daughter. If a reason can't be identified, try to track the emotional changes that occured and see if they could be related to hormonal changes. Help your daughter understand these patterns too so that she doesn't feel so out of control when they do occur. Emotional extremes may also be related to sensory issues, or to judgments that your daughter experiences because she's not wearing the "socially acceptable" fashion at school or engaging in "gender appropriate" games and activities. It's important to identify, as far as possible, the reasons for her struggles, so that you can help her come up with effective solutions.

If you are an adult who experiences similar emotional situations, identifying them for yourself can also help you find a concrete reason for the changes in your mood, emotions and behaviors. When we know what causes these changes, we can feel more in control because we are able to anticipate them and also come up with solutions to minimize the impact or exposure to these situations.

Special interests, if they are present, are a great way to help a female Aspie feel successful. Their interests are things that are extremely important to them, and can be used to help build self-esteem, and confidence, and also to help them show their skill and intellect to others. In the neurotypical world, high value is placed on social competence as a way to be successful in life. Individuals on the autism spectrum tend to value their intellect in the same way. Special interests and skills can also be important tools in helping a female Aspie calm down when they have had a difficult experience or a hard day. If your daughter is still in school and struggles to transition home calmly, providing her with some time to engage in her special interest before starting homework may help the transition feel more successful, both for her and for you.

At the end of the day, having a diagnosis on the autism spectrum doesn't mean there is something wrong with you, or your daughter. Having a diagnosis on the autism spectrum doesn't mean that you are broken and it doesn't mean that you need to be fixed. It is something to be understood, respected, and embraced, by you and by others. Yes, there are skills that female Aspies may find harder to learn in order to function successfully in an NT-dominated world, but these are skills that can be learned and supported so that you or your daughter can feel successful in the world you are living in. If you are someone on the spectrum, or someone who loves a girl or woman on the autism spectrum, take the time to understand their world as much as they need to understand yours. Love them and cherish them (or yourself) and appreciate the uniqueness and value they bring to your life and the world around them.

FURTHER READING

BOOKS AND E-BOOKS

Asperger's and Girls

Tony Attwood and Temple Grandin

This book shares the stories of professionals and women on the spectrum as they navigate through experiences of school systems, puberty, transitions to work or college, and careers.

Aspergirls

Rudy Simone

This book takes the reader on the journey of a female on the autism spectrum using the author's own experiences as well as the voices of over 35 women on the autism spectrum.

Pretending to be Normal: Living with Asperger's Syndrome

Liane Holliday Willey

This book shares Liane Holliday Willey's personal story of her life and the struggles she faced growing up as an undiagnosed woman on the autism spectrum. It wasn't until adulthood that she finally received her diagnosis.

Safety Skills for Asperger Women
Liane Holliday Willey

This book focuses on the physical and emotional safety of women on the autism spectrum. Liane Holliday Willey describes the pitfalls many women with Asperger's may face and suggests helpful ways of overcoming them.

Thinking in Pictures: My Life with Autism
Temple Grandin

Dr. Grandin's personal story of her life with autism and how she managed to overcome many barriers in the world to become a highly successful woman with autism and a professional in her field.

WEBSITES
Asperger Women's Association
www.aspergerwomen.org

Dedicated to women who have been diagnosed on the autism spectrum, the website includes a blog and a variety of other resources.

Aspie.com
www.aspie.com

This website is created by Dr. Liane Holliday Willey to celebrate the differences and experiences of individuals on the autism spectrum.

The Autism Society

www.autism-society.org

Provides information on state support groups that can help individuals and families with treatment and diagnosis, and gives information on autism spectrum disorders.

Autism Spectrum Australia

www.autismspectrum.org.au

Information on diagnosis, early intervention, and other treatment services for individuals and families on the autism spectrum.

Help 4 Aspergers

www.help4aspergers.com

A website by Rudy Simone dedicated to providing information and support to women on the autism spectrum.

Icare4Autism

www.icare4autism.org

The International Center for Autism Research and Education provides information, news, and opportunities for involvement through donations, volunteer opportunities and writings for women on the autism spectrum.

Irlen®

www.irlen.com

The Irlen® Institute specializes in identifying light sensitivities in individuals and the brain's difficulties in processing visual information successfully. The website includes information on the diagnosis, the symptoms, and how they can help. It also includes a self-test to determine if Irlen syndrome may affect you.

The National Autistic Society

www.autism.org.uk

Information about autism for individuals and families in the UK, including living with autism, schools and services, and working with individuals with autism.

Oasis

www.aspergersyndrome.org

Information and support for individuals with Asperger's syndrome.

Wrong Planet

www.wrongplanet.net

A website for individuals with Asperger's to talk about various topics with others on the autism spectrum.

INDEX

autism spectrum disorders (ASDs) *cont.*
  uniqueness of females with
    18, 86, 113, 155
avoidance
  of family gatherings 24
  in interpersonal situations 9–10,
    31–2, 45–6, 155–6
  as protective factor 32
  when being bullied 71, 118

birth control 151
black and white perspective
  42, 46, 65, 156
brain 36, 51, 86, 92, 94, 115,
  149, 157, 161
bullying
  Alison's experience 56–60
  cyberbullying 61–2
  depression as consequence of 68, 156
  differences in experiences of
    NTs and Aspies 70–1
  emotions experienced as result
    of 65–6, 67–8, 70–1
  excluding and ignoring 63–4
  experiences of reporting 66–7
  female Aspies as targets for 62–3
  having lifelong impact 60
  in many forms 60
  oversensitivity towards
    emotions of others 109
  passive-aggressive 69
  PTSD as consequence of 71
  self-harm as consequence of 68
  and stimming behavior 118
  taunting 65, 67
  tools and support
    for adults 76–7
    for children/teens 72–6
  in the workplace 58–9, 68–70

careers 119–20, 133–4
clothing
  for comfort 92, 126, 131–2, 136, 138
  fashionable 64–5
  "girl only" or gender neutral
    131–3, 136
  and sensitivity to touch 82–4,
    92, 125–6, 139
communication
  as anxiety-provoking
    experience 34, 46

different facets of 27–8
different style of 30–1
difficulties arising due to people 27
girls using more subtle 129
link with social interaction 27
made up of unwritten and
  unspoken rules 46
nonverbal 27–8, 33–9, 54, 89, 156
of NTs 30–1
practicing 75
preference for concrete 31
tools and support 53–5
translating information for 88
and verbal teaching 89
see also social interactions
compliance 11
control
  of emotion 44–5
  of external environment 41,
    43–4, 101, 133
  lack of, over bodily changes
    141–4, 146, 148–9, 150–1
  music for sense of 116
  over physical contact 84
  over routines 121
  practicing, to give sense of 34
  rituals to gain 109–10
  and self-harm 68, 76, 146–7
  of social experiences 11, 133
  stress and anxiety caused
    by lack of 41, 107
  time limits for sense of 51
  of voice 33
  when engaging in special
    interests 45, 119
conversations
  with co-workers 23–4
  ending 55
  with family members 24–5
  feeling left out of 28
  fluid movement of 47
  nightmare of 26–7
  practicing 32, 34–5, 75
  problems with "art of" 10
  socio-emotional content 28–9
coping and adjustment strategies 9–10
cyberbullying 61–2, 68, 73

depression
  animals for reducing 74
  as consequence of bullying 68, 156